Flying With
The
Rich and Famous

(True Stories from the Flight
Attendant who flew with them)

By

Patricia Reid

A new, funny, up-lifting, light hearted take
on what it's like to fly around the world
with the rich and famous

This book is dedicated to the most amazing parents a girl could ever ask for. I was lucky enough to be born to parents who taught me what I needed to know about life. They taught me to love whole heartedly and to be nice. I had a phenomenal childhood and I love them dearly. Thank you mom and dad. Plus they believed in me - that I could write this book!

And to my son RJ, who I can always brag about because he always gives me reasons to brag. I call him brilliant because he is. He's so brilliant! And we're not British. I love you my brilliant baby. And I literally could not have done this without his brilliant brain.

And to my pseudo-brother Ross, may you rest in peace. I can't wait to laugh with you again. Love you bro-ski.

Contents

Chapter 1: As the Prop Turns

Chapter 2: Sky Roads

Chapter 3: As the Jet Rotates

Chapter 4: What Goes Up Must Come Down

Chapter 5: Another Day in Paradise

Chapter 6: Welcome to Life on the Road

Chapter 1: As the Prop Turns

How I Came to Be a Flight Attendant for the

Rich and Famous

I grew up in Huntington Beach, California, also known as "Surf City." I was blessed with phenomenal parents and two incredible older sisters. We didn't have a lot of money, but we had a lot of fun. We went waterskiing and snow skiing and camping and flying. My father is a pilot and has always had a Beechcraft Bonanza. (Dad still does "fly-bys." We run outside when we hear the distinct sound of Sheila's engines and jump and wave at him. He dips his wings when he sees us as if he's waving back—we've been doing this forever!)

By the tender age of four, thanks to my father, I already knew what I wanted to do with my future. On Saturdays, Dad and I went flying in his four-seat Beechcraft Bonanza, nicknamed Sheila and dubbed his "mistress." He would bring telephone books for me to sit on because I couldn't see out the window. When I got older, he would move the yoke (steering wheel) over to my side and let me fly. I loved flying with him.

We often took Sheila from Long Beach, California, to Catalina Island—appropriately named the "Airport in the Sky"—to have a famous Buffalo Burger. When we flew over our house and the beach, I would giggle to myself how the people looked like ants. We flew over Disneyland and Knott's Berry Farm and I laughed that the people on the rides had no idea what a better ride I was having above them. Occasionally, Dad would rent a Cessna 150 and we would fly upside down and do crazy-eights, zig-zagging the sky.

We took trips as a family in Sheila, too. We would stop at a quaint, little airport called Nut Tree in Northern California on the way to see relatives. Nut Tree had a charming, multi-colored train that would take us from the tarmac to the neighboring town, through the walnut trees and the village where there were lots of candy and nut stores—and then stop in front of the toy store! I couldn't wait to go there or anywhere actually. It was during one of these excursions I realized what I was going to do. I was going to become a stewardess, as they were then called. I loved to get on a plane, destination anywhere, just to be somewhere else, to experience something different.

By the time I began high school, my impatience to become a flight attendant had increased. My best friend even wrote in my yearbook, "I hope your dreams of becoming a stewardess come true." Was there ever a question? Of course they would come true. And since I knew exactly where I was headed, well, not exactly where, why did I have to wait to finish high school? I was a straight-A student, and I was in a hurry—let me out! One of my teachers told me about a proficiency test, similar to the GED. I took and passed it when I was sixteen; I was officially a high-school-proficient-adult. Although I hadn't even reached my junior year, I begged my father to let me go to

3

our local community college.

At Orange Coast College they had a flight service program designed for girls like me. I desperately wanted into the program, and the sooner the better, but my father insisted I return to high school for my junior year. I harassed my poor dad constantly until he either couldn't take my badgering or decided that college courses might teach me more than I was learning in high school—they did. We compromised: I would take mostly transferable courses and a couple of flight-service courses. I entered OCC for the spring semester. At sixteen, I was the youngest student on campus, and I was thrilled.

During my second year at OCC, a new airline was being conceived. Jet America was to utilize the underused airport at Long Beach, California. I immediately applied to be a flight attendant, but I was hired as a ticket agent. I was now eighteen and in charge of my own life, and decided to leave OCC to begin my much-anticipated career.

On a cold November morning, Jet America Airlines opened with two flights per day to Chicago, O'Hare. I spent an extra hour getting ready that day. I slept in rollers the night before, so my long dark blonde hair was all curly and wild. I put on gold eye shadow to bring out the green in my eyes and put an extra coat of mascara on my already-long eyelashes. I painted my lips red to match my blouse then squeezed my five-foot-five-inch frame into my size four navy blue tunic dress. I was ready to begin my journey.

Jet America heavily promoted the convenient location of Long Beach Airport, which was adjacent to the 405 freeway. Our first flight ticket fares were $4.05 one-way. What marketing! The return flight was $45.95. When I arrived at the airport that first day, there was a line at the ticket counter a quarter-mile long. No one knew it was going to be so popular, but people had camped out around the terminal and down the street.

Our printers were not yet up, so we handwrote tickets;

none of us were very good on the computers, so the line crawled. I stood on my feet for three days handwriting tickets, having slept in the manager's office on the first night because people were irritable and grouchy from waiting. It was crazy, confusing, exhausting and exhilarating.

I knew immediately this was where I belonged; I loved the passengers and the interaction with them. I talked to everyone, treated my frequent fliers like royalty, and became best buddies with anyone who worked in the airport. My father taught me the value of remembering a person's name, advice that has served me very well over the years.

Because I was so good with the passengers, I was put in charge of lost luggage. I didn't even mind if people were screaming at me when we had indeed lost their luggage. Nor did I mind when someone asked me for the fifth time that day what time our eight o'clock flight left the next morning. We had a trailer for the holding gate, and if the flight was late, I would play games with the passengers. They loved it, and I loved it.

While happily working away at Jet America, a passenger came through my ticket line, and my gregariousness impressed him. As usual, the flight was delayed, so I was playing games with the passengers in the holding gate. He struck up a conversation with me and then he asked me if I had ever thought about becoming a flight attendant. Are you kidding me? Yes, yes, yes, I had thought about it! He asked if I would be interested in flying for a new airline, Regent Air. I could barely contain myself.

Regent Air was a first-class-service-only airline with three Boeing 727s reconfigured with only thirty-three seats. They had two daily scheduled flights from Los Angeles, California, to Newark, New Jersey. On Saturdays, there were no flights. The concept was to compete with American Airlines, TWA, etc., for first-class passengers, except that Regent Air was vastly more lavish and opulent, like a whole new class of service, where the affluent were treated with the utmost care and respect. Regent Air intended to spoil their guests to the *nth* degree.

The passengers were collected at their homes and chauffeured to the airplane via limousine. On arrival at their destination, they were again chauffeured to their hotel or other destination in New York or Los Angeles. The same service was done in reverse for their return. There was no terminal, no security, no waiting; the luggage was loaded in the limousine at their homes and unloaded directly onto the airplane. It was a novel idea.

Each plane was exactly alike. There were six club seats and a couch in the first section, then the bar-galley section with three club seats and a love seat. The last section had a row of four club seats across, and behind them were four private staterooms. Each of the staterooms contained four club seats that converted into beds, and there were curtains at the entrance that could be drawn closed. Beyond that, a barber's chair sat across from an extra-large, very plush lavatory—that lav was used for an array of things beyond just a toilet. Because it was so big, many couples went in there for hot sex, keeping it locked for far longer than need be. It was also a popular place to light marijuana joints, snort lines of cocaine, swallow pills and/or whatever else the passengers had with them. It was well used, as were the staterooms.

The interior of the airplanes were luxurious and exorbitant, yet soothing and comfortable. There were swarms of deep burgundies, mauves, and royal blues throughout the club seats and headliners. The carpet had variant shades of burgundy, mauve and grey that swirled around in a flowing pattern. The bar was brass with burgundy leather, and the etched Plexiglas mirror behind the bar flaunted peacock feathers. The partition between the bar-galley section and the last club seat also sported etchings of peacocks posed in opposite directions. The outside of each aircraft was painted blue on top and white on bottom with two gold stripes. The insignia on the tail was back-to-back gold Rs with a gold crown on top.

The cuisine and amenities were as exclusive as the passengers. The menu included Maine lobster, Beluga caviar, and Taittinger champagne. We used real silver cutlery, fine Irish linens, delicate Spode china, and Baccarat crystal stemware, all done with flair worthy of the rich and famous.

Each flight attendant was hired for a specific position. The chief purser was in charge of the cabin and the other four flight attendants. The food and beverage specialist worked behind the bar, pouring and mixing drinks and preparing the food. The cosmetologist was to give haircuts and manicures. Finally, the executive secretary took dictation and assisted businessmen if they chose to work onboard.

I was hired, after three interviews, as a secretary, although I never once did anything remotely similar to a secretary. With great pride and anticipation of what lay ahead, we all wore black tuxedos with burgundy bowties and cummerbunds.

The first few flights were not very full, but we took no notice. We would arrive in Newark after gorging ourselves on all this incredible food, which was intended for the phantom persons who had yet to discover Regent Air, and head straight into New York to party like the rock stars they assured us would be forthcoming.

As word of mouth spread, things started to liven up. We amassed a guest list of film stars, television stars, rock stars, singers and songwriters, politicians, publishers, sports figures, producers, Wall Street gurus, and prominent businessmen. Every flight was full, and every flight was an adventure with the rich and famous. I looked forward to each takeoff with such anticipation that nothing could have dampened my spirit; this is what I was meant to do, and I was having the time of my life.

Regent Air never charged enough to sustain itself, so it

was only a matter of time before the numbers didn't add up; inevitably, bankruptcy ensued. After being laid off, I did stints of waitressing and went back to school. (Dad was right. I needed something to fall back on.) Eventually, I became antsy being grounded and looked for a way to get in the sky again. I considered commercial airlines, but I was a first-class flight attendant. How could I do the "chicken or beef" gig? I went to airports and knocked on doors in search of elusive private jets that I had overheard the passengers on Regent Air talking about. I went on a mission to land myself on one or hopefully, many.

I eventually discovered a woman who offered a service like a brokerage for private flight attendants. The clients would call her for a flight attendant for so many days; she would supply the flight attendant and take a percentage of the daily rate. I was tenacious and would not take no for an answer. She finally acquiesced to my relentless requests and gave me a chance to prove I could do this, and do it well.

I spent the next two decades flying around the world on an array of different jets for an assortment of corporations and individuals. Some years were very busy, and I was never home. I missed holidays—I awakened one Christmas morning alone in a suite in Hawaii; I also missed any number of weddings, milestone anniversaries, and cherished family vacations. Some years were slow. I would have to subsidize my income any way I could, usually by driving limousines.

But to this day, every time I buckle myself in and we are sitting at the end of the runway preparing for takeoff, I'm truly excited to hear the initial roar of the engines winding up their powerful turbines preparing for our blast into the sky. I suppose it's the anticipation of the unknown, and it's at this moment I am truly peaceful. There's never been a doubt that I am where I am supposed to be.

Chapter 2: Sky Roads

What a Private Jet Is Really Like

Business aircraft have been in use for years, but most people are not aware of their existence, let alone the magnitude of their impact. Beginning in the early 1900s, corporate flights were started by a farmer's innovative aviation interest. He built a plane out of wood and fabric and flew it from the Mississippi River to the Rocky Mountains. Then, the end of World War II contributed to the transformation of military jets to business jets.

There are roughly 11,000 business jets in the world, mostly in the United States. A private jet can be of enormous value, mainly because of the freedom it allows the owners to go where they want when they want.

There are many different types of business and personal aircraft. They range from a small plane like Sheila- my father's

Bonanza, all the way up to large jets like the airlines fly. Some fly even farther and faster than the airlines. The airplanes I fly are roughly the size of a motorhome. They are tall enough to accommodate a six-foot man and vary greatly in width and length.

The movie studios have fleets of jets, and some have jets on both coasts, ranging from helicopters all the way up to the "big dog" airplanes. If the studios are promoting a new film and the film stars are going on tour, they might take one of the jets. Sometimes they take a mid-size jet that would not have the need or room for a flight attendant, but if it's across the country or overseas, then they take the large jets, the Gulfstreams and Challengers, the jets that I fly.

Many celebrities, like John Travolta have their own jets. He's a plane enthusiast, and he has had a Gulfstream, among other aircraft in his private fleet, for years. Tom Cruise, Donald Trump, Bill Cosby, and Oprah Winfrey, just to name a few, all have private jets. Many major corporations own jets—American Express, Hewlett Packard, Disney, Wells Fargo, and Sony, for example and there are many, many more. In addition, a great number of wealthy individuals have private jets, some renowned and some low profile. And let's not forget Air Force One, which is any plane the Unites States President is in but usually a Boeing 747.

Just like anything else, private jets vary in price. A brand new Global Express or Gulfstream can cost upwards of fifty million dollars. An older Gulfstream or Challenger can be picked up for under ten million dollars – but watch out - some of them will break down all the time, some of them are too noisy for popular destination cities, and some of them are major gas guzzlers!

A corporation purchases them mainly for business use. If a major corporation has a meeting in a rural destination that takes three commercial airline legs (number of connecting flights) and six hours to get to, they are certainly going to take their own private jet that will get them there in two hours. Or if they have to be in Europe on a specific date and time, they are again going to take their own aircraft. Not to mention it is safer for the CEO of a major corporation to be with his private security on his private jet than on a commercial airplane. Plus they can get a ton of work done on the way and have a much better dinner! They also use them for vacations and other side interests and hobbies, or they may "loan" them to their friends who have a special need for a private jet – this is the case when I get "loaned" too. They also loan them to the Make-A-Wish Foundation and other philanthropic organizations.

Then there are companies that obtain them in order to charter them for a hefty fee. Let's say you are a regular private jet customer and your regular private jet charter has chartered all their aircraft that weekend. You want to take your new date to San Francisco for the weekend (think the movie *Pretty Women* here). The charter company will call everyone they know in order to get you a jet. *"Sorry we don't have one available"* is not an answer! Private jet charter is a very viable and lucrative business when the economy is good, however not so much when the economy is bad. Look at the last ten years...

Then there are those individuals who just have a lot of money. These guys – or gals, are usually a blast to work for. Normally, they are very easygoing, drama free, down-to-earth, kind and sweet as the day is long, etc. - *usually*. Some of them can be the most demanding pigs on the planet. I have always been lucky with these kinds of owners, really lucky. Almost all of them have treated me so incredibly wonderful - as you will learn later on. All are different to work for within the realm of corporate aviation.

A corporation-owned aircraft is often more desirable from the crew's point of view because, plain and simple, they have more money. The almighty dollar—yen, euro, yuan, franc, riyal, pound, real, posada, peso—is a vast consideration in this business. It affects airports, transportation, fixed base operators (FBOs), hotels, catering, pay, everything, which affects our jobs and the passengers we fly.

A charter outfit either owns the jet outright or manages it for another company or individual. It's relatively common for a corporate or individually-owned jet to charter when it's not in use, to offset the cost. Just parking an aircraft overnight can cost more than $2000 depending on where you are in the world. The management or charter operation can provide everything for the jet, including crew, maintenance, and inventory or they can provide nothing but shelter. A huge benefit to working charter flights is the tips. A charter client will often tip the crew - some of the tips are an outstanding bonus on top of our regular pay.

Having a private jet available to you and your desires is a profound convenience for those who can afford it. It's profound to me, and I have to work the flights! There's no security, no timeframe, except for those pesky cities that have noise abatements and don't want a forty million dollar dog whistle awakening their residents at three in the morning. There's no one to tell them "no" to anything. If they can pay for it, they can do it. They can drive their car or limousine right up to the airplane, get out, get on, and go away. Well, they do have to take two pilots with them. They can take a flight attendant or not, or a flight engineer/mechanic or not, up to thirteen (some hold more) of their best friends or not. They can take twelve strippers and a monkey if they want!

These airplanes are kept at fixed base operators, or FBOs. This is where the airplane fuels up, gets catering, maintenance, a bath, or whatever else it needs. They're usually located across the tarmac from the terminal or at one end of the runway. Some aircraft are housed inside the hangar (airplane garage) and some outside. Passengers start and end their trips at the FBOs if the airfield has one. Some airports have a few FBOs and some have none.

When you first step aboard a private jet, it's awe-inspiring. It is truly the ultimate in travel, sophistication, comfort, elegance, and spaciousness. There's plenty of room—room for everyone to spread out and get comfortable and do so in the most luxurious surroundings. You might become aware of a crisply dressed flight attendant standing in the rear, waiting to meet your every desire, and two cocky pilots—oops, I meant competent pilots—tending to your luggage before they whisk you away.

These airplanes have long, sleek lines of striking wood panels and large plush club seats surrounded by exquisite head and sideliners and custom, fire-retardant carpeting. The club seats are on either side of the plane and there's an aisle down the middle from the cockpit through the passenger cabin, galley, and into the lavatory (although, some have forward galleys and/or lavs). These jets are sparkling clean and neat like a formal living room, but once in the air they can morph into a quaint theatre, a cozy bedroom, a five-star restaurant, an important boardroom, or a lavish celebration, all while soaring through the sky at 500 miles per hour.

No two jets are alike. Unless ordered from the get-go by a corporation, they are all completely different, except that they're all fabulous. There are many options in the interior configuration. Besides the inviting club seats that recline and swivel, there might be a stylish divan where a weary traveler can stretch out and read a book or have it made up into a bed for a serious snooze on Egyptian cotton and cashmere. There can be a four-top table, fundamental for a vital meeting or a rowdy game of poker—way fun!

Some airplanes have a credenza overflowing with fresh flowers, an abundance of appealing snacks or the latest issues of the world's leading magazines. A larger private jet might have a full-size bed and maybe even an entire bedroom. Let me tell you, lying on a bed as you lean and sway with the airplane is the ultimate in sleeping pills. The lighting and music can be adjusted to create a comforting and peaceful ambience, especially at night.

The galleys are a gleaming combination of polished wood drawers and cabinets and lighted, overhead partitions where the crystal stemware hangs. These gorgeous galleys blossom into gourmet kitchens with everything one needs to prepare a mouth-watering meal at 35,000 feet. They carry exquisite china and cutlery and unique wares for all sorts of ethnic creations. In the rear of the jet is a beautiful, over-sized lavatory with all the necessities one can imagine.

The resources used on the inside of these deluxe modes of travel vary greatly. I have seen one hundred percent goose-down-stuffed seats, baby-soft lambskin-covered seats, the finest ultra suede head and sideliners, raw silk head and sideliners, twenty-four carat bathroom fixtures, exotic wood cabinetry and paneling from the depths of the Brazilian rainforest and even granite galleys, which are very expensive due to weight. The carpet is usually quite unique with maybe a company logo or pattern of some sort in the weave. I have seen crystal so delicate and thin that, if you sneeze, it breaks. The linens on a private jet can be of the utmost quality, so fine and expensive that it pains me when one spaghetti dinner reduces them to rags. I have folded the softest cashmere blankets and hand washed exquisite silver cutlery. I have also hung the most outrageous full-length fur coats and gawked over large diamonds that would barely fit on a perfectly manicured finger.

Operating the stereo and DVD equipment on an airplane can be the most trying challenge on the planet or as simple as using a car stereo. One aircraft I flew had such intense stereo/DVD equipment I felt I needed an engineering degree just to turn it on, let alone get it to function. On a favorite Challenger of mine, if the DVD wouldn't play, you would have to bang on the bulkhead behind it, and then, magically, it would come alive. I have found that the best eclectic crowd-pleaser movies to have

24

on hand are the classic Johnny Carson Tonight Show interviews, especially when a few people onboard are waiting for late arrivals (someone is always late). It's difficult to be irritated while you're watching Dean Martin, Sammy Davis Jr., and Frank Sinatra in all their glory. A motto for my life would be "Hurry up and wait!" because that's exactly what the crew does. I have waited for passengers for hours and hours and hours and hours. I am not exaggerating – we as a crew once waited six hours for a family to show up. We were told every hour that "they were on their way." They actually did show up – no kidding – six hours late. And we still had to fly a five hour flight. Never forget your book in this industry or you will go stir crazy!

When a private jet is ordered, we have to design the interior configuration, deciding whether the galley should be forward or aft and what it will include. Some galleys are very small and hard to work, and some are large and equipped with most everything you need to please even the most finicky connoisseur. We have cold storage like a refrigerator, but it's the outside air blown in that keeps it cold. We have standard ovens, microwaves, coffee makers, and toasters. There's hot and cold running water and some have instant-hot spouts that deliver boiling hot water in minutes (a huge help with tea drinkers). Some sinks are small and it's nearly impossible to do dishes in them, and some are large and take up too much counter space, which is usually sparse to begin with. Depending on owner preference and logistics, we may do all dishes onboard or none; they can be given to the FBO to do for us – we usually let the FBO's do them for the sanitation purposes. There have been times when I had no choice but to do the dishes in a bathroom sink in the middle of nowhere - you do whatever it takes. There are ice bins for clean ice and ice bins to keep the sodas, water, beer, and wine cold - aka- dirty ice. We have pantry-type space and we carry a smaller, vastly more expensive version of what's in your kitchen right now.

I designed a couple of galleys I thought were pretty darn close to perfection, but everyone has an opinion, therefore every galley is completely different. The only standard in the industry is that there is no standard. Some galleys make sense while you're working them, and some you might be moaning about the whole time: that the trash bin is in a stupid place or the ice drawer is too small or the coffee maker is hard to get to, or, or, or—every flight attendant bitches about something in the galley.

One aircraft might be perfectly organized and one might be a haphazard of nonsense everywhere. Inventory has no rhyme or reason from one aircraft to the next. Even if you've flown a particular airplane before, the next time you come aboard it might be completely rearranged. Every flight attendant thinks her way is the right way. So, when you're on descent and it takes a while to find the hot pad to remove the cookies from the oven, the cookies slowly slide to the front of the baking sheet, creating some very funny-looking cookies.

The private jets I fly carry only the finest quality products available. Standard issue includes fifty to one-hundred-dollar bottle wines as well as premium liquors, nuts, chocolates, and designer water. The cuisine can be spectacular! Usually, we order a selection of food we'd like to serve from the finest caterers in the city we're in. We can order just about anything, and the caterers deliver the food directly to the aircraft, where I will arrange it to meet my in-flight needs. These catering bills can be staggering, jaw-dropping expensive, but the result is outstanding. I almost always have a fruit and cheese tray or a crudités platter for nibbling, on top of all the dry snacks we carry (no munchies left behind). Basically, I am the purchaser, hostess, maître d', line cook, waitress, busboy and dishwasher, and high speed snack technician. Let's not forget nurse, safety guru, and your-way-out in the event of an emergency.

By the way, we go through emergency training just like the airlines. Some of our training is more intense than the airlines and some is simpler; it really depends on the company but we can sure as heck save your life if we have to. I had one chief pilot that chartered a boat in Newport Beach harbor. We had to do a mock ditching (landing in water) in the freezing cold water. We had some crazy guy from some survival company that made us jump over the side of the boat. Then we had to use all our training to get back to the boat – like it was a raft. That was one of the worst days of my life - it was so cold that all my blood had gone to my organs leaving my arms and legs useless. I had to take off my jeans and throw them over my head to "catch" air in the legs and then tie the legs in a knot, creating a flotation device. That was so damn difficult, trying to tie the knot before the air escaped out of the legs. I think it took me more than twenty times to do it properly, so my jeans actually allowed me to float upon them, but it did work. Then he made me swim back to the boat even though I had floated away from it, way far away from it, remember I had no use of my arms and legs. I don't really know how I got back to the boat. I hated my chief pilot that day. I didn't talk to him the entire way back to the marina. And he just kept laughing; they were all laughing at me. I did not think it was funny, not in the least. Actually, I don't think I talked to him for a week. But, now you all know how to survive in the water with a pair of jeans!

Some companies carry really expensive equipment onboard that will relay a passenger's medical issues (once I hook you up to it) to an emergency doctor on the ground. The doctor can see what the passenger looks like and read all the vitals. He or she can tell me what the passenger needs to stay alive until we can land. In all my years of flying, I have never had any major medical or emergency issues—knock on wood! The worst thing that ever happened to me was running out of vodka on the way to Europe! But as luck would have it (depending on how you look at this), we had a minor mechanical issue and had to temporarily land in New York. I immediately and secretly tipped a ramper to go and get me vodka…whew.

Although, as far as close calls, once on Regent Air, four Wall Street stockbrokers shared a stateroom. They were all drinking red wine and chatting. It was a quiet, dark night and I remember hearing idle conversation and the hum of the engines. Everything was status quo and then bam! Out of nowhere, we hit a wind shear and dropped about 1,000 feet in a nanosecond. Just like that. It was like God stepped on us, and then immediately realized he was stepping on us and removed his foot.

We went straight down, then straight up, it felt like the floor had fallen out beneath my feet. I happened to be walking in front of the stockbroker's stateroom when this happened. I flew straight up out of my shoes as did the wine right out of the stockbrokers' goblets; then I came right back down as did the wine in the glasses. I was stunned - the stockbrokers were pale. Then all four of them immediately pushed their wine glasses to me to pick up for them. Well gee, I thought to myself *"yes, I'm ok, thank you for your concern!"*

A day in the life of a private jet passenger might go something like this. You ascend the stairs, and I settle you into a seat of your choice. (If you're not the chief passenger, you best be going to the back of the bus. He who pays the bills gets his choice of the frills!) I begin by bringing you a glass of sparkling champagne or the beverage of your choice, served on a shiny silver tray – I usually have a sprig of mint and/or a small flower on my silver tray as well. I then bring you a superior selection of newspapers and magazines and offer a cozy blanket and pillow, sometimes even a cashmere sweater and slippers. Usually, I have a boarding snack basket or fruit bowl set up on the credenza for you to peruse while waiting for everyone else to board. I also have "boarding music" playing - that choice depends on who I'm flying and where we are going.

After we are in the air, the full meal service starts. I pull out your table and set it up with fine linens and silverware. I pour wine into your glass, which will never go empty, and serve you course after course of mouth-watering cuisine. The meal service might last hours and include up to six courses. After all, you've no place to go. I might start with a unique appetizer, then a crisp salad or homemade soup, perfectly warmed bread and butter, your favorite entrée cooked exactly the way you like it, with vegetables of the ideal crunch. Finally, of course, a decadent dessert served with premium alcohols and gourmet coffee.

I really love to serve dessert and most of my passengers enjoy it on their flights. I mean, you're on a private jet—who cares about calories right now? I have a homemade secret recipe for oatmeal chocolate chip cookies that I bake onboard. I will make the batter at home then bake them in-flight. I also order one hundred percent pure vanilla ice cream from the caterer which is brought to me on dry ice. (Dry ice is a hazardous material but in small amounts is fine, as it dissipates anyway) After I bake the cookies, I make an ice cream cookie sandwich with the vanilla ice cream – but you have to be very careful on timing. If you take the ice cream off the dry ice too soon it will be hard as a rock and break a tooth. Too late and it will melt all over and make a gooey mess. Sometimes, I will roll the ice cream sandwiches in mini chocolate chips. Many a pilot has coveted these cookies, making every burn mark on my right hand and arm worth it. It's always fun having your arm in the four hundred degree temperature oven and then hitting turbulence - essentially, these airplanes are two-ton, forty million dollar, five hundred miles-per-hour Easy-Bake ovens!

Another one of my favorite desserts to prepare is hot fudge sundaes. The ice cream is once again packed with dry ice, and I purchase all the condiments before departure. When you receive a loaded hot fudge sundae on an airplane in the middle of an eight-hour flight, in the middle of a dark ocean, it's impossible not to take thorough pleasure in every bite. Just ask the pilots.

If we're in a foreign city, I like to serve food that's indigenous to the area. For example, in Fort Lauderdale, Florida, I immediately think stone crab claws; in New England, definitely clam chowder and lobster. In the South, barbeque is a must. I do a lot of cold seafood platters because everyone loves them, and a chicken caesar salad is usually a perfectly acceptable choice for lunch.

There are times, especially on long trips—say over the center of the Pacific Ocean in the middle of a dark night—when someone might be craving a peanut butter and jelly sandwich and a glass of milk. Or maybe in their inner time zone when its morning and they want breakfast. I have done fried eggs, bacon, and toast many times after the passengers have awakened from a long sleep, and we still have a way to go. I've also prepared and grilled tuna melts for pilots who were longing for comfort food and home.

Some passengers like to have their catering from one of

their favorite restaurants, so I will order and pick it up on my way to the airport. One of my favorite owners loved king crab legs from a famous seaside eatery, so I would arrange dinner from there often. One of my favorite pilots loved a salad dressing from an old, well-established Newport Beach restaurant, so I would always bring that with me when we flew together. I have been sent on missions for favorite meals from the most alluring establishments and famous restaurants that I couldn't wait to see, and I have been sent on wild goose chases for items that were so hard to locate that I would pretend it was a scavenger hunt.

Some passengers bring something special with them. Sometimes it's a person, like their personal chef—nothing like getting it your way! Wolfgang Puck designed all the cuisine for Regent Air, and I have had personal chefs prepare the food for a specific flight. Early in my career, one woman brought all these paper bags from a famous restaurant with her for lunch. She handed them to me and said "Please prepare our Steak tartare for lunch." Now I was all of twenty-something and grew up camping and flying in Sheila; I had *no* idea what Steak tartare was! I asked the pilots – they were completely useless. I didn't have a clue what to do with all those condiments. Steak tartare is minced raw beef (superior quality beef) with onions, capers, a variety of spices, Worcester, and usually a raw egg (but in this case it was hard boiled) all rolled up together – or something like this, depending on where you're getting it from. Since I had no idea, I served each condiment in individual ramekins. Well let's just say, that woman was not too happy with me that day! I don't think I ever flew when she was on board again, but I did fly her husband.

Occasionally, the owners or pilots will request the flight attendant purchase everything at a high-end grocery store and prepare it fresh onboard. There's been some flack over this by the FAA as the flight attendants are not allowed to prepare food on a charter aircraft. Regardless, no matter where the food comes from, before every departure I shop in my home city; staples are a necessity. Most dry goods are stocked on the airplane already with backup stored in the hangar. At the very minimum, I will purchase fresh-squeezed orange juice, half and half, milk, bread, lemons for water, limes for beer and cocktails, flowers, newspapers, magazines, and whatever else I deem necessary for the duration of the trip. Running out of something during the flight is not an option—it would be problematic to stop at 7-Eleven.

If you are flying for a foreign company, let's say a Japanese company, then you must shop at a Japanese grocery store. Trying to translate the language so you can buy the appropriate videos, snacks and the periodicals can be very challenging. Trying to get a hold of those Japanese newspapers in Oklahoma is *almost* impossible. You must pre-arrange all of this before you leave on that trip. You cannot expect a business man from any culture to not have his favorite newspaper on his own private jet, no matter where you are. Usually, they want

three or five newspapers on the credenza when they walk in the

jet – almost always, the newspapers are the very first thing they

grab, even before they give me their suit coat. Many times, they

don't have time to read them on that particular flight, but they

will take them to the hotel and read them there. As their flight

attendant – you *best* be having their preferred newspapers!

There are exceptions, of course, to decent catering. An

out-of-the-way airport in the middle of rural Arkansas or a small

town in a foreign country can prove to be quite the challenge.

These destinations require a flight attendant to plan and prepare

ahead. Sometimes, one encounters language barriers and/or

misunderstandings. I once ordered tuna-stuffed tomatoes from a

handler (handlers sometimes replace FBOs, usually in foreign

countries) in Taipei, Taiwan. I intended them to be prepared as

entrees; however, when they were brought to the airplane, they

were tuna-stuffed *cherry* tomatoes and not nearly enough to feed all my people. As luck would have it, I had the easiest going passengers on that trip and I just added my own canned tuna and made tuna sandwiches for lunch – nobody cared – but it could have been a nightmare with other types of passengers. (Now you see why I bring staples – I needed the bread for the sandwiches!)

There have been plenty of times when I received catering at the aircraft, and it was just not worthy, especially for the price. I have pitched a fit or two and absolutely refused the food unless it was prepared to my standards. The caterers will call their kitchen in a panic and have the food remade to my liking, then drive back and pick it up. This doesn't happen very often but when it does, it really freaks me out. Occasionally, the passengers will show up and I'll be in the back receiving the replaced catering through the baggage door. This situation seriously unnerves me – I strongly dislike not being prepared in advance, especially in this career. But it can happen – sometimes the caterer is just late. Once again, late is not an option in this business!

Many times, we'll enter the United States or a foreign country at an airport where we can refuel. The pilots, depending on weather, fuel reserve, customs and immigration availability— and whether or not they need more Guinness from Ireland— ascertain this fuel stop. After flying all day from Europe back to the United States, the passengers might just want a cheeseburger. These entry cities and fuel stops are occasions when I have sent someone to McDonald's for us. Hey, the rich and famous eat like everyone else and who doesn't crave a Big Mac now and then?

At that time, most private jets did not have the capacity to fly from the West Coast to the Pacific Rim or Europe without a fuel stop. If going west, we would almost always stop in Anchorage, Alaska. If going east, we usually stopped at Bangor, Maine or Reykjavik, Iceland. Sometimes we spent the night, sometimes we changed pilots, sometimes all the crew changed and sometimes we'd bring on another pilot and keep going.

Although, now the newer aircraft can make it across both ponds without a fuel stop, depending on the route, winds, etc.

Anchorage is very accommodating to business aircraft, passengers, and crew, and they have outstanding catering. Of course, they're making some serious money with the amount of fuel we purchase.

Once, we were taking off out of Anchorage heading for Japan. I had served a huge breakfast to everyone, as it's a long flight across the Pacific. About a quarter of the way through the flight, breakfast began to hit everyone in the gut and the lavatory was being used frequently. The odor began lightly but escalated to an overwhelming stench. I tried to spray air freshener but you know how that is, it just smells like daffodils and daisies on a dairy farm. My chief passenger decided he could take it no longer and asked us to dump the lavatory.

We landed in some remote part of Russia. It was so unreal—the dilapidated buildings with only three walls, dirt and gravel in between. The bland landscape, such pitiful nothingness, it looked like left over ruins from a long ago war, yet it was a usable fuel stop. It truly made me appreciate where I lived. Landing that airplane to dump the lavatory had to cost an immense amount of money, but I must admit it was worth it.

Incidentally, many of these take-offs and landings I am usually in my jump seat between the pilots. But a passenger can sit there too, if the chief passenger and the chief pilot agree on this. Many, many times I've put passengers in my jump seat when there was something very special to see – Russia wasn't one of them, at least that part of Russia. But Alaska, well Alaska is stunning!

As I've mentioned, when traveling around the world, I always bring staple food with us. Once when we landed in Perth, Australia, the agriculture inspector came onboard to confiscate all the food like they usually do. Most country's including the United States confiscate food when you go through Agriculture upon entry into a country. They usually burn it; this is standard procedure in most countries if not all of them to keep foreign bugs, pests and disease at bay. It is how they keep disease and pests from spreading around the world – think about that for a minute. Anyway, Australia is known for being more severe about it. That inspector stole my mayonnaise. The mayonnaise was not opened and the seal was intact. I was not about to let my mayonnaise go. How was I going to prepare a tuna fish sandwich if my boss wanted one? We still had a long trip ahead of us, and I might need that mayonnaise. I argued with him, he argued with me. I was pissed—he was pissed. Then my chief pilot stepped in and said, "Patty, let the mayonnaise go." At that point, I looked up at my pilot and I realized I had to let the mayonnaise go, but as I am writing this, I am pissed off all over again.

And speaking of food, I can't tell you how many disgusting things I've tried around the world. That Vegemite stuff from Australia is just gross. Apparently, it's their equivalent to our peanut butter, uh—not! And crocodile—mind if I barf? Kangaroo—where's the toilet? Rabbit—that's just not right. Snake—couldn't pay me enough. Eel—no, thank you. Puffer fish—hmmm, shall I risk dying today?

The one common denominator in flying the rich and famous is the constant change in itinerary—and I do mean constant. I've had flights change more than twenty times before we actually departed, probably more. Everything can change: destination, passengers, airports, hotels, anything and everything. I never count on anything until I look the chief passenger (decision maker) square in the eye, and even then you're almost guaranteed it will change again. I've been summoned at 7 p.m. for a 7 a.m. charter going to South America (I made it, great trip). I might be sound asleep in my hotel room and get a call that the passengers want to leave as soon as possible. You just never know. It's a good thing dispatch doesn't call the crew every time something changes or we'd never actually fly! Due to the number of people the information is transferred thru, it can become very convoluted. If the crew is the last on list, and we almost always are, we might get to the airplane at our normal one and half to two hours before departure only to discover the passengers are waiting to depart. Uh...oops!

I've also re-positioned several times for charters and owners alike. Let's say the aircraft is in Illinois and I'm in California. I get paid to fly commercially from my closest airport to the closest airport in Illinois. Literally, all I do is go to the airport and get on a plane, they pay for the ticket, transportation and my daily rate. Then I'll work the trip, getting paid my daily rate and do the same in reverse when the trip is over. Since I love airports, this is like heaven to me - getting paid to travel!

I also used to commute to San Francisco a couple times a week for a company who couldn't find a full time flight attendant. It started only because this company needed a flight attendant the next day and couldn't find anyone. So I did it. They ended up liking me, so I flew up and down the coast for several months while they interviewed other gals. I became good friends with all the United Airline flight attendants, so they upgraded me most of the flights!

The norm for me though is a nice, polite couple who just want to get to Hawaii or the Caribbean for their anniversary. They're not demanding in the least and just want a light lunch and/or maybe a few cocktails. Then they give me a nice tip before landing and say, "See you in a week!" My two favorite pilots and I head off to a luxurious hotel where we have a fantastic week off on the company's dollar, thank you very much.

Ok, all you wanna-be private jet flight attendants getting your resumes together—don't bother. The industry is saturated with laid-off and experienced private flight attendants, not to mention the scores of commercial gals. Besides that, the competition is fierce and as cutthroat as one could imagine. But heck, I made it!

Chapter 3: As the Jet Rotates

Celebrity Flights

With chartered flights you never know who your passengers will be, whereas with a corporation or individual you've flown with before, you'll probably know their likes and dislikes. For instance, some owners will get pissed if you serve them "designer" lettuce or maybe they dislike tomatoes or something of that nature. And you can run into the brand problem if you fly for a corporation. For instance, if you are working on an aircraft that belongs to a food corporation, then you cannot put on any item that is in competition with those companies' products.

You may get a bunch of spoiled rotten kids, or a group of ornery, ill-mannered adults, or a plane full of obnoxious drunks. I flew a slew of men once where every guy was so plastered that

49

they harassed me mercilessly and endlessly. They were becoming extremely inappropriate, so I begged the pilots to increase the cabin altitude—therefore, reducing the oxygen level—until they all passed out. On a charter for a wealthy television executive, I believe this was King Distribution, the chief passenger had ordered individual seafood platters for each person and then he ate his off the floor while lying on the couch!

I flew a charter for three men that had four "working girls" with them. They pretty much locked me in the cockpit the entire time. I really didn't need to be there at all, but some charter outfits won't send their 30 million jet anywhere without a flight attendant. This flight was the nastiest I had seen, or rather, heard. I heard, as did the pilots, way too much! It was kind of like; I want to listen, but it's disgusting and I shouldn't, but I'm curious. All three of us ended up listening as best we could.

Then again, you might get lucky and have the best group of people ever and get a handsome tip to boot. You might have the name Mike Smith as the chief passenger on the manifest, but, in reality, it'll be a celebrity or person of interest. It truly is like a box of chocolates, you just never know what you're going to get! My line of work is not predictable, not in the least—you must remain flexible, and you'd better adapt or risk being grounded.

PRESIDENT RONALD REAGAN

One of my fondest memories is having the unbelievable honor of flying the late former President Ronald Reagan. I was told that this flight was "donated" for a goodwill event, something that some corporations will do. This goodwill flight was my good fortune, as I always believed President Reagan to be a visionary.

President Reagan was first an actor, appearing in more than fifty feature films. He eventually became president of the Screen Actors Guild, which led him to politics and a run for governor of the great State of California. He won that election and stayed for eight years. Then Reagan achieved the greatest goal when he was elected the fortieth president of the United States and leader of the free world. He again served two terms and was widely respected and esteemed for creating eight years of peace and prosperity. He was definitely a most memorable presence in the White House.

I arrived at the airport hours beforehand, not wanting to miss any activity. It was an early morning flight and there was to be no food service, so the only thing I could think to do special for him was make some really great coffee. I went to my favorite high-end grocery store and studied the choices. I ended up with a vanilla bean roast, but when I made it on the airplane, my chief pilot nearly had a coronary. "Presidents don't drink flavored coffee!" he exclaimed. I quickly poured it out and made the old standby: Starbucks.

When President Reagan arrived at the aircraft, not surprisingly, he was flanked by Secret Service, but what was surprising was that employees working at the FBO were everywhere. It was shoulder-to-shoulder people staring back at me. This was a moment that no one wanted to miss. Gossip flies through aviation quicker than the Concord across the Atlantic—but, still, I couldn't believe how many people were there to witness a United States president exiting a limousine to board an airplane. It couldn't have been more than a three-minute show.

President Reagan climbed the stairs to the aircraft with his Secret Service agents and a few aides. Although he was beginning his golden years and was somewhat frail and slightly hard of hearing, I could see the wisdom in his eyes. I wanted to ask him questions—you know the kind of questions that are so beyond finding an answer to, ones I felt only President Reagan would ponder. All I could manage to get out of my mouth was, "Would you enjoy a cup of coffee?"

As I served him, I learned he was going to San Diego to deliver a short speech. We spoke briefly and somehow he turned my stumbling conversation into his genuine gratitude for the ride. I marveled how President Reagan, considered by many to be one of the greatest presidents of the twentieth century, was so sincerely grateful for a ride!

When we landed in San Diego and he began to make his exit, he made a point to thank me again and shake each of the pilot's hands and thank them as well. He was the most dignified person I've ever flown and undeniably the one I most respected.

TOM CRUISE

I received a call for a three-day charter on a Gulfstream out of Van Nuys airport. This was one of those years I was really busy. I didn't feel like leaving so soon after my last flight, but when I am called, I go.

My first clue this might prove to be a very interesting or possibly difficult flight came with the laundry list of catering and shopping requests. The next clue should have been that I had been given two-day notice for this flight, instead of the typical two hours. That turned out to be a good thing given the obscurity of the list; it took me that long to locate everything. Plus the catering requests were all different; everyone had asked for something eccentric and dissimilar.

Finally, I learned my passengers were Tom Cruise, his producers from one of his films, and various other hotshots. Tom Cruise! I was especially eager to meet him and anxious to bestow upon him the best possible service. While awaiting his arrival, I fluffed and re-fluffed pillows, smiling like a cartoon character and thinking how much fun the next three days were going to be.

Our first flight was five hours to the East Coast to scout movie locations. Immediately, it was apparent that the producers and assistants considered themselves genuine VIPs. They began barking orders as soon as they arrived. "Where's an outlet for my laptop?" "Hang my coat up and don't let it get wrinkled." "I'll take some water, no ice, with lemon." "Do you have my pulp-free, fresh-squeezed orange juice?" They were all shouting commands and questions at the same time and without so much as a please or thank you; and they all talked over each other, like each one was more important than the last. I felt like I was surrounded by a bunch of five-year-olds.

While I was running around with a wrinkle-free coat on my arm, pointing at outlets, answering questions and serving drinks, the man who felt he was in charge—whom I dubbed "Mr. King Bowtie" to myself—said, "We are in a hurry and need to take off immediately." I thought, *Maybe if you weren't over an hour late, Mr. King Bowtie, we'd be on time!* I secured the cabin for takeoff while everyone glared at me, perturbed that I didn't ignore the pulled out tables with the contents of their carry-ons strewn everywhere. Exhausted, I sat down for takeoff. Uh-oh. This charter was going to be *work.*

Well before the captain turned off the seatbelt sign, the barking began again, except for Tom. What made me notice him was that he extended me the basic courtesy of "please" and "thank you." That and, of course, his huge, warm, comforting Tom Cruise smile.

While constantly running to and from the galley, meeting demands for more pasta for one guy, separate plates for another, and trying to determine how fruit should be cut to qualify as "bite-sized pieces," someone stumped me with the complaint that his chicken wasn't "pink" in the middle. *Wow. Sorry sir, not serving salmonella today.* I glanced at Tom who smiled sympathetically. Momentarily, I was caught in his glow, but it quickly passed when someone yelled, "No ice, with lemon."

Finally, the meal service was over and I had cleaned the galley. Frazzled, I poured myself some coffee, and then I heard from the passenger I dubbed Mr. Tighty Whitey, say: "Stewardess, I'm still hungry." *Mr. Tighty Whitey, you better get some bigger undies, 'cause I just fed you, and about that stewardess word...* (A stewardess works on a yacht).

Meanwhile, Tom Cruise had taken his food and drink

57

anyway it came out of the galley. Because he was so easy to please, I ended up giving him better service than the rest. I don't know if that was an unconscious "rub" to the other passengers, or because he was Tom Cruise. Whichever, he deserved it for being the only gentleman. He even asked, "How do you remember who is drinking what?" "How can you carry all those dishes in high heels?" "What if we hit turbulence, won't you topple over?" I laughed and thought, *Well Tom, vanity trumps practicality.*

After food service and a tiny bit of calm, Mr. Tighty Whitey asked me to remove the brown M&Ms from the candy dish! I stood there totally bewildered. I opened my mouth to speak, but nothing came out. So, I said to myself: *Fine, Tighty Whitey, OMG! I feel sorry for your wife. I'll remove them.* I went into the galley and began to throw M&Ms into the trash, missed and flung them all over a forty million dollar galley, not even caring that maintenance would read me the riot act for littering in their baby. Unbelievable. What the hell is wrong with these people? Only when I realized that I hadn't washed my hands, did I crack a smile. My mouth took on a maniacal grin and I began to chuckle, just thinking of all the disgusting oozing germs I hoped I was getting all over his candy. Then, in the midst of my breakdown, I looked up and saw Tom Cruise snickering at me. Our eyes met, and I knew he understood.

When we finally landed, I was toast. I needed to get to the bar to "debrief." I'd barely said "boo" to the pilots during the flight. I think I threw them a sandwich along the way, but that's not how I normally treat my pilots. With all of our lives dependent upon them, they're gods and I treat them as such, usually spoiling them tremendously. As we sat in the bar the whole ugly story came pouring out as the pilots listened sympathetically.

Most pilots can tell quickly if the passengers are going to be egocentric, ill-mannered "problem children." They were not surprised to hear my harrowing tale of the "alpha-hotels"

59

(airplane talk for a-holes). But we all agreed that Tom was in the wrong company because he was cool, by far the nicest guy on the flight. At least, *his* mother would have been proud of him.

After sipping expensive martinis—thank goodness for expense reports—I went to my room for some well-needed R&R. We had a short flight the following morning. Mr. Tighty Whitey reminded me there was to be a full-meal service. Anxious about the next day, and on East Coast time, it was difficult to fall asleep at a decent hour.

After little sleep, I put two packets of coffee in the little coffee maker and reminded myself it didn't matter how these men treated me. Their rudeness is about them, not me. I normally love driving to the airport, seeing the beautiful plane, brewing gourmet coffee, heating cinnamon rolls, playing inviting music, and making it homey. Usually, I can't wait to greet my passengers with a level of enthusiasm that might sometimes be over the top. But not this time.

As soon as they boarded the plane, the flight quickly became a repeat of the previous day, only in fast-forward. We only had an hour of flight time, so I really had to hustle. After the pilots "dinged" me (fasten seatbelt sign), I hastily raised tables and delivered beverages. They all ate something different again but I was undaunted. Eight meals prepared in a galley the size of a hall closet—no problem. With a full passenger load, halfway through the meal service, the first few need beverage refills and it snowballs from there. When I set the last entrée plate down, it was clear that Bottom-of-the-totem-pole-Dude had to eat in a hurry. He had been pretty easygoing the day before, probably as I figured it, because he knew his rank. But now he decided he was at least important enough to bitch about being served last and while on descent. *Sorry, B-O-T-P-D, someone has to be last.*

Now it was time to face the inherent problem of a full-meal service on a short flight: dishes and glassware all over the cabin. The galley had stuff everywhere. It looked more like a

61

greasy spoon rather than a luxury airplane, and we were landing. I frantically picked up dishes, glasses, crumpled linens, and papers, in addition to trying to secure briefcases. All of a sudden, and totally unexpectedly, Tom Cruise jumped up to help.

At first I was appalled: passengers were not supposed to help, certainly not Tom Cruise. Apparently he didn't care about his status. He bussed dishes from the cabin into the galley, but he did it with a child-like demeanor, laughing and joking the whole time. He was amusing and entertaining everyone, especially me, as I gratefully took the dishes from him and recklessly shoved them into dirty dish bins.

He was cute and funny and a huge help. I forgot who he was for a moment because he was so much fun. It was like doing dishes with your brother on Thanksgiving, except this brother was a superstar.

As I'm flinging things here and there, it dawned on me: Tom Cruise was my busboy! I began to giggle under my breath.

That egged him on. He had changed the whole atmosphere of the airplane from tension to absurdity, at least for me. He started teasing me about how the crap all over the galley was stowed. "Where was it to start with?" "How does it all fit?" "Where's the dishwasher?" He was so adorable and silly that for the first time on this charter I noticed I was enjoying myself.

As landing was imminent, I insisted he sit down. It really wouldn't look good if he went flying through the cabin in the event of a hard landing. I sat down just as the wheels hit the tarmac.

I sat there sweating, thankful that Tom was sitting forward and not in my line of vision. I was embarrassed about his helping me, even though he did seem to enjoy it. But what most captivated my thoughts was how the others could go through life acting like spoiled children. It was at that moment I realized I had the unique ability to go where the paparazzi couldn't and to see what a person is made of when no one is watching but the flight attendant.

After distributing all the coats and carry-ons, something odd happened. Mr. Wrinkle-free Cashmere Coat thanked me. After I picked myself up off the floor, I had to laugh. The day before, they deplaned without as much as a glance back. Then it happened again. Bottom-of-the-totem-pole Dude thanked me. I thought, *Sure, smarty-pants, you just don't want to be left standing there without jumping on the thank you bandwagon.* But, I have to admit, some of them became a little nicer. Maybe seeing Tom bussing tables warmed them up. Then Mr. Tighty Whitey actually complimented me. Holy cow, where's the defibrillator?

After spending hours cleaning up a totally disheveled airplane with the help of my pilots and a shocked ground crew, I left the airport knowing Tom Cruise was really the star of this whole show. And if he and I were pals, I didn't have to give a hoot what the producers thought anymore. I was once again excited to be the flight attendant extraordinaire.

When they arrived for the next flight, they showed more respect, except for Mr. King Bowtie who was still an alpha-hotel. Some even asked about my time off, but Mr. King Bow Tie never looked me in the eye or said thank you. This was the first time I saw an example of real "Hollywood" behavior that most people only hear or read about.

It wasn't the last time I had flights like this. I just do my best with the limitations that exist while soaring through the sky in a metal tube.

JACK NICHOLSON

One of my all-time favorite passengers was Jack Nicholson. He's always been a diehard Los Angeles Lakers fan and would often fly back and forth from Los Angeles to New York on Regent Air to follow them. His courtside antics were always newsworthy. People love Jack. Everybody was enthralled with him, everyone wanted to meet him, sit next to him, chat with him, anything with him. Jack has been a popular movie star for decades, but at this time his ride to stardom was just beginning, having won one of his Oscars for his crazy portrayal of McMurphy in *One Flew over the Cuckoo's Nest*.

He became a familiar and friendly face, and one I always looked forward to seeing. He was an extraordinary guy with a grin that could light up a room. What I remember most is his signature Ray-Ban sunglasses. I don't think I've ever seen him without them. When I first met him, he had chartreuse-colored Ray-Bans that matched his chartreuse-colored socks. I don't know if he matched his Ray-Bans to the socks or his socks to the Ray-Bans. Either way, it was cool and only something that Jack Nicholson could pull off.

His voice is sexy and soothing, and, well, comforting— like a long-proven friend or a valued mentor. Whatever he says seems monumental because Jack Nicholson has that voice. Every flight attendant wanted to wait on him or hang with him or just be around him. I will never forget his words or his wisdom—or his flirtation.

Jack radiates immense self-confidence, a laid-back enthusiasm and sexual energy. Adding to his singular good looks and amazing attitude was his smile. He was always smiling and in a sexy way that isn't designed—it's just the way he is. Not to mention you can tell he does not give a crap what anyone thinks. He's the most authentic person I've ever flown with. Let me repeat: he is the most authentic person I've ever flown with.

Everyone told me Jack was a big flirt so you'd think I'd have been prepared. But when he flirted with me, everything people said went out the window. It became personal. Even though Jack often traveled with his nephew, when he flirted with me, it was like we were the only two people on that airplane.

I remember one particular flight, early on, that especially had my heart racing. When Jack first boarded the aircraft, he handed me his coat. When I took it to hang in the closet, he thanked me in his sexiest voice while locking in on my eyes for what felt like an eternity. It was a hypnotic stare and one I hated to break. When I brought him his first drink, he touched my arm, and it electrified my entire body. (Or maybe it was the static from the airplane, but I doubt it.) When I went to remove that drink for takeoff, he again thanked me in that sexy voice while his eyes pierced mine—and then he smiled a tiny little grin where his lips curl up just a tad on the sides of his mouth. I felt like he wanted me to be his lunch that day.

After takeoff, I brought him a fresh cocktail, and he began his little quips. He'd say the funniest one-liners with just a hint of sexual innuendo. Then at some point during this flight he got up to go to the bathroom, and he had to pass me on his way to the rear of the aircraft. The aisle was narrow there so he brushed up against me, and we locked eyes again. He stood there for just a smidgeon longer than needed. He said something, but I can't remember what because I was too fixated on not fainting. The repartee playing in my head was annoying. I was almost considering taking this bait—but, was it bait or was it just Jack?

Let's just say that Jack Nicholson got some seriously good service on that flight. I offered him anything and everything on the plane, except me. I wonder how obvious it was that I "over-serviced" him. I hope he got a kick out of it. I know I did.

ELIZABETH TAYLOR

The late Elizabeth Taylor was no stranger to private jets. The beautiful actress had a lifelong career and was queen of the tabloids. Dame Elizabeth Taylor, Cleopatra herself, famously married eight times—really, eight times! Starting as a child star and rising to the epitome of success, she was the ultimate movie star. I would venture to guess that she was the most recognizable face in the world. Plus, she was a philanthropist. What she did for HIV/AIDS was unprecedented.

The first time I laid eyes on her I was stunned at how truly beautiful she was in person. I had seen her on the big screen and television, but film did not do her natural beauty justice. She was stunning. It was like seeing her in high-definition. She was absolutely gorgeous. And then I noticed how petite she was. I had envisioned her larger than she was, maybe because of her star status or maybe because of her larger bust.

Elegantly, she climbed the stairs to board our beautiful 727 in a full-length, white fur that was the most spectacular coat I'd ever seen. I've been trained never to show any sign of being star struck and usually had no problem mastering it, but her coat made me gasp. As she strolled through the airplane she held her head high. She seemed to be very comfortable with her stardom, as opposed to those celebrities who would come aboard wearing dark sunglasses and enormous hats, as though that would conceal their identities. She acknowledged any staring eyes with a polite nod or small eyelash wink as if to say, "Yes, it's me—I am

Elizabeth Taylor," and "Yes, you may gaze upon me." I felt that it was okay with her if we stared, not because she was vain but because one couldn't help it. Curiosity is a natural instinct and she was okay with it. My initial impression was that she wasn't a diva, unlike some celebrities I had come across.

I was very intent on getting a closer look at Elizabeth Taylor's violet eyes, but Ms. Taylor was sitting in another flight attendant's section, my dear friend Felicia. She was as excited as the rest of us to host Elizabeth Taylor on our flight but more exuberant because she was in her section of the aircraft. Felicia took Ms. Taylor's magnificent coat to hang in our aft closet. When she got to the rear of the aircraft, a few of us were waiting to see the coat and hear what Felicia had to say about her.

Felicia told us that she asked Ms. Taylor how she was feeling that morning, and she had replied that she was in fact feeling marvelous, to which Felicia responded, "Well, if you feel half as good as you look, you must feel fabulous!" To which Ms.

Taylor responded, "That is the nicest thing anyone has ever said to me!" Then Felicia blurted out to us that Ms. Taylor was wearing *the* diamond: the famous Richard Burton diamond. The 69-carat pear-shaped diamond he had given her during their first marriage. (She married him twice.) Each of us instantly conjured up ways to get a closer view of her hand.

On examining the coat, we noticed the inside was silk and had "Elizabeth Taylor" embroidered on it. One of the flight attendants was a rather flamboyant gay man named Stephen, who was just a gas. He had a way of making sure we kept our status, in his perspective, equal to the celebrities. "We are just as good as them," he would constantly remind us, and usually in some hilarious fashion.

Stephen decided he should try on the amazing garment and see if he could *feel* what it was like to be Elizabeth Taylor. When he did, the sleeves came only just past his elbows and the hemline only to his knees. The sight of him turning that coat into a gag was funny enough, but then he began dancing in the back of the airplane pretending to be the extraordinary star. He had his head cocked to one side, his arms waving and he pranced around as though he were in a sketch on *Saturday Night Live*. It was such a comical sight that Felicia and I laughed so hard we had tears rolling down our faces. It took us forever to regain our composure and touch up our makeup so we could return to the cabin and tend to our passengers.

As the flight proceeded it became apparent that Ms. Taylor was taken by Felicia's compliment. When Felicia returned, she politely admired the diamond, which was when Felicia learned that is was not the famous Taylor-Burton diamond but the 33-carat Krupp diamond that Richard Burton had also bought her. (She had sold the Taylor-Burton diamond to fund a hospital.) Ms. Taylor promptly removed the exquisite jewel from her finger and told Felicia to try it on. When she saw Felicia's reaction, she insisted she wear it—for the entire flight!

As if Felicia didn't have enough bragging rights because Liz Taylor was in her section, she now had this massive diamond to flaunt in front of all of us and the other passengers for the next five hours!

It wasn't until much later, when the meal service was winding down, that I finally had an opportunity to speak with Ms. Taylor. I found her eyes to be what everyone said: utterly unique and striking. They were the most unusual color blue that I'd ever seen—a deep rich hue, lined with dark cat-like rings and black lush lashes that made them appear violet. They seemed to pierce your soul, yet with warmth and integrity. They took my breath away, truly. When I refilled her coffee she looked up at me, touched my arm and said thank you with sincere gratitude and a quick bat of her eyelashes. She said how wonderful it must be to fly for such a lovely airline, to which I responded, "Well, it certainly is with charming people like you aboard!" She was extremely beautiful and extremely kind, very personable, warmhearted, and well mannered. She was definitely one of the finest celebrities I've ever flown with.

What left a lasting impression on me was watching Felicia squirm out of one of the most famous diamonds in the world to return it to its rightful owner. She had captured much attention wearing it, and she wasn't giving it back without an audience. With childlike fun she milked taking off that ring for all it was worth. We all began to chuckle as she very slowly inched it up her finger, pretending it was too tight and needed to be precisely maneuvered. Even Ms. Taylor was enjoying this little show. When Felicia finally returned the exquisite ring, many of us began clapping. I wrapped my arms around my friend as if to say, "It's okay, missy, there'll be another ring someday!" After we all said goodbye to Elizabeth Taylor, we talked about how much we loved her, especially the way she embraced her fame and the responsibility that went with it.

ROD STEWART

75

When I realized that I was going to be flying rock star Rod Stewart, I was thrilled beyond belief. My sister has had a thing for the sexy rock star since I can remember. She played his *Every Picture Tells a Story* album over and over and over again. I mean, I know every word to every song on that album. To this day, he is on her to-do list—you know that list we all have where if the moon falls from the sky and <insert celebrity crush here> wants to "do" you, you get to. So, I'm thinking I've got major bragging rights here. Not to mention he began his wild ride to fame while I was still in high school, so his music is like home to me. Does anyone listen to "Maggie May" without singing along?

Rod Stewart came on the airplane a little tipsy with a sexy swagger and a "cheerio" smirk upon his face. I swear he was a walking, talking advertisement for his song, "Do You Think I'm Sexy?" Yes, Rod, we think you are.

He was a happy-go-lucky guy. He had every right to be— his career was rock solid and climbing. He was very thin and had a head of hair that was blond and wild like the cartoon character Lisa on *The Simpsons*, except it wasn't drawn in yellow crayon. His outfit was, however, like yellow crayon—very bright and eye-catching, and, believe me, he caught everyone's eye. He was dashing. Then he spoke to me in that delicious accent and it all came together, *Forget it, Sis, if the moon falls, I get first dibs!*

He was exaggerated in every way. He asked for a cocktail right away and continued downing them one after another. Each cocktail brought him to an even more cheerful place. He was animated during our brief, delightfully amusing conversations. We had an easygoing repartee, and he was easy to please. As he drank, his accent became more and more pronounced and by the end of the flight, I could barely understand him.

But with the outfit, the hair, and the personality, I was loving life and grateful for the opportunity. He was the kind of celebrity that didn't require much attention, and he was very considerate. I had a marvelous time flying across the continent with him, and I secretly hoped to have the opportunity to serve him again.

And that I did, shortly after our first flight. When he came aboard, I could tell immediately that something was different. His whole demeanor had changed. There was no animation this time. He was quiet and reserved. Maybe he needed a cocktail, I thought. But when I asked him for his choice of beverage, he requested "fizzy water."

What the heck is fizzy water? I wondered to myself. He must have seen the surprised look on my face because he quickly explained that fizzy water is sparkling water. Oh, thanks for the clarification, maybe he's just thirsty. Or maybe he's preparing his kidneys for the upcoming festivities. I anxiously awaited the call for alcohol, but it never came. He drank only fizzy water. No alcohol at all.

He seemed much more "British" on this flight and a wee bit shy. There were no bubbly conversations—no bubbly of any kind. He kept to himself and was very quiet. I was bewildered. I really didn't get it. Maybe his cat just died. Maybe the cleaners ruined his yellow coat. What had happened to Mr. Wonderful? It was very strange.

As I tended to the other passengers, I noticed Rod looking at me with a weird expression on his face. When I approached him, he began to chuckle. He seemed to know something I didn't, and it quite amused him. I thought he was going to start drinking, but then he told me that he was on "week off."

"Excuse me? What do you mean 'week off?' I asked.

He explained that he lived a week-on/week-off lifestyle: one week he drank, and the next he didn't. Wow! Thank you! Mystery solved! I explained my confusion to him, and he broke into heartfelt laughter. I served him another fizzy water and went back to my role of fervent fan and first-class flight attendant. Now that I understood, he was the man sitting on the moon again (please Rod, gain some weight, so the moon will fall). The duration of the flight was awesome. He was much more chatty and lively even without the alcohol. Polite and easy-going, he smiled at me a lot. I adored him. What a rock star role model Rod was.

DOM DELUISE

I love to rollerblade on the boardwalk in Newport Beach, California, where I lived, cruising along, listening to my music and inhaling the scent of the ocean and sand. One sunny day, just as I was lacing up my boots, I received a phone call. It was disappointing to have to stop what I was doing and pack a suitcase, but that's the way this lifestyle works. When I read the manifest, however, I was happy to trade in my rollerblades for a set of wings. Movie and TV star Burt Reynolds had booked the charter for him and his friends.

Unfortunately, Burt was not feeling well, so we were told to monitor him without intrusion. We sat Burt in the very rear of the aircraft where he could have peace and privacy, and he was subdued for the most part.

One of the guests on this charter was comedian Dom DeLuise. Dom and Burt were best buds and often co-starred in various film and television projects, usually comedies. Dom had a reputation for being funny—really funny. I had read that movie shoots took longer when he was involved just because people couldn't stop laughing. So, I was expecting this to be one hilarious flight.

Dom boarded the airplane with a huge smile on his face and introduced himself to everyone, shaking each person's hand vigorously and thanking us before we even did anything. He was very exuberant, gregarious, and excited to be on the flight. He made me feel like we were all lucky to be alive and on this airplane together because we were going to have so much fun. While I escorted him to his seat, he linked my arm, waved the other hand with a lively gesture and said with a jovial flourish,

"Show me the way!" When we got there, he gave me a bear hug, so huge it consumed my entire being. After I caught my breath, I thought, *this flight is indeed going to be memorable.*

When we settled at our cruising altitude, Dom pulled out a huge pile of paper. It was his personal stationery that read: *From the desk of Dom DeLuise.* Next to that there was a small caricature of him, with a gigantic grin, naturally. He told me that he wanted to send Burt a note to cheer him up since he wasn't feeling well. He scribbled something on his letterhead and stuffed it into a matching envelope. He then shouted that he needed a delivery boy for his "air mail." Singer and songwriter Paul Williams (another in this boys' club) jumped up and ran over to Dom to volunteer.

They made a big production out of Paul delivering Dom's "air mail," saying how important this letter was, and that it had to be hand-delivered. It was so very funny, everyone was giggling.

Paul got down on his hands and knees while Dom

"knighted" him for his role of emissary and sent him on his way to "deliver de letter." Still on his knees with Dom's "precious cargo" in hand, Paul began to inch his way to the back of the airplane while chanting, "Hear ye, hear ye." Everyone was in hysterics. He was taking his role as the knighted postman seriously! When he got to Burt Reynolds, he formally announced that he had an "air mail" delivery for him but proceeded to sort of toss or drop the envelope in Burt's lap in a lackluster way. At this point, the laughter drowned out the jet engines.

Maybe the vigorous audience around him fueled Dom, because he continued to write letters to the other celebrities onboard. It was becoming mayhem throughout the cabin because "air mail" was "flying" all over the plane.

Then Dom decided that the pilots needed a letter, too, and again jotted something down. But he'd fired Paul Williams as his delivery boy—something about delivering letters to the wrong people. He proceeded to reprimand Paul, scolding, "You're just

83

like the postman delivering the wrong mail to the wrong addressee." And guess who he wanted to replace him? Me, that's who. He shoved me off to the cockpit with a letter for the pilots after lecturing me on how to deliver his mail correctly, then pointing to the front of the airplane and instructing me: "That's where the pilots are." (Ok, I'm blond but still!) When I got inside the cockpit, I opened the letter for the pilots. It read: "Do you know the way to Tampa Bay?" We all cracked up because we were in fact headed to Tampa Bay.

The comedy sketch continued as we flew across the entire country. As the mail wound down, Dom found new ways to keep us entertained. He came up to the galley where we had balls of butter out in a bowl and said, "Yum, butterballs!" He popped one into his mouth—without the help of bread or water, just a giant ball of fat—then he looked at us for a reaction and with a hearty laugh meandered back to his seat. He was constantly "on," and never has five working hours gone by so quickly. Other than

84

Burt not feeling well, this charter was one of my favorites.

SYLVESTER STALLONE

We were all thrilled to find out Sylvester Stallone was one our passengers, but we had one flight attendant who was especially excited. This woman was so over-the-top exuberant over Sly I thought she might start hyperventilating. She was so ridiculously star-struck I wanted to slap her. Seriously, she was driving us all nuts.

When Rocky Balboa swaggered into the cabin, in all his gorgeousness, we kind of saw where she was coming from. He was extremely handsome, buff, and seriously sexy. If you looked into his eyes (which turned out to be a rare occasion), you were frozen; his eyes are the epitome of being "lost in those eyes." And when he spoke in that distinct mesmerizing voice, I was almost ready to jump on the loony flight attendant's bandwagon.

I was really expecting some kind of Rambo persona, like

he would save the airplane and all of us in it if the flight went down. But after just a few moments, the bottom fell out of the airplane and the air out of my lungs—I very quickly realized he didn't give a hoot about anyone but himself. He didn't acknowledge anybody, passenger or crewmember, and he never made eye contact with anyone. The only time I saw his eyes was when he first boarded the aircraft. He rarely spoke and when he did, he would ask for something in as few words as possible. His tone was flat and cold, like it was an effort for him to move his lips or his head for that matter. He said what he wanted and that was that: we were dismissed, like we were the help or something. Okay, we were, but still. It seemed like he felt as if he had the whole airplane to himself, like he was traveling alone (which he wasn't), like he was the king of this flight and everyone else were his subjects, or like he owned the airplane (which he didn't). I was really surprised because he's such a good-looking man and plays "Joe hero" type of characters, but in real life he

86

was exactly the opposite.

Thank goodness, Miss Loony Flight Attendant had him in her section (a gift from me) and gushed over him repulsively. I kept my distance. I did learn that preconceived notions have no place in this business. Makes you wonder how many other erroneous mental pictures we have in life. Forgetting rules and regulations, Miss Loony asked for Sly's autograph and was never invited back because of it.

GOLDIE HAWN

Some of my flights on Regent Air were noisy and rowdy, especially at night. The passengers would be drinking and partying, chitchatting with one another and excited to meet another celebrity or person of interest. It was entertaining to watch the dynamics: who thought they were better than another, and who wouldn't be caught dead talking to whom.

The bar/galley area was the core of all the entertainment.

If a passenger was in one of the three seats in this section, sleep would prove difficult if not impossible, and privacy was out of the question.

Goldie Hawn was a last-minute addition on a Regent Air flight. The lovable, comedic star is usually cast as the typical "dumb blonde." She's certainly anything but. However, she's always played it to a "T"—remember *Laugh-In*? Always a huge, silly grin upon her face, many people were enamored with Goldie, especially television and film producers who knew she could bring in the male viewers on variety shows that were all the rage in the eighties. She then moved on to critical acclaim as a movie actor and a respected producer. Her political and personal beliefs have also made her a unique soul and someone most women admire—if nothing else, out of jealousy over her twenty-five plus year romance with Kurt Russell! And, of course, she is mother to Kate and Oliver Hudson.

The plane was at capacity, except for one seat right next

to the bar, and I could tell this flight was going to be a perpetual party across the Great Plains. Goldie was late and the last passenger to come aboard. When she did turn the corner from the stairs into the cabin, immediately everyone became calm and quiet, which I would have thought was bloody impossible with that crowd. The other passengers were looking at her in awe and admiration. You could tell they were filled with intrigue and curiosity. Of course the only seat left was that one in the middle of the "war zone."

Known for her sunny disposition, on this night she told me she was dead tired and just wanted to be left alone. She pleaded with me to find her another seat. Unfortunately, nobody was willing to give up his or her coveted seat. When Regent Air became the popular way for celebrities to travel, the unique seating configuration became an issue—some seats offered more privacy and were therefore more desirable. I could not find another place for her and so there she sat like the proverbial fish in the fish bowl with everyone staring at her.

And wouldn't you know it—all of the sudden, everyone needed a drink refill, so off to the bar car they went. The people, who had no qualms or a lot of wine, or both, decided they would have a little tête-à-tête with the talented and adorable Goldie Hawn. I believe more people were enamored with her than all the other female celebrities put together (except perhaps for Elizabeth Taylor). She was as polite as possible but I suspect she was thinking, "Get the hell away from me!" Just because someone is normally the cheery, sunny-side-up kind of gal, doesn't mean they're always that way. It didn't take a rocket scientist to realize she didn't want company, I felt so sorry for her—people can be such ignoramuses.

As soon as we took off I gave her some earplugs, a blanket, and eyeshades and told her to pretend she was sleeping. I don't know if she got the rest she wanted, I don't know how she could have with all the prying eyes. I couldn't believe how people were gawking at her. They were checking her out like she was a new car they were considering. How I wanted to give them a piece of my mind, but obviously that wasn't an option. These passengers made the paparazzi look like amateurs.

JULIE ANDREWS

I have flown many children—children who had a nanny or nurse or one of each to look after them. And I have flown children who had no one to look after them. I have flown spoiled brats and downright disturbing delinquents. For every flight that has children aboard, I brace myself with patience and empathy. Most kids just need some love, attention, and boundaries, I think. Sometimes, this helps more with the parents than the children!

Early in my career I was thrilled to have Julie Andrews and her two adorable, adopted little girls on a flight. No nanny. No nurse. No assistant. No manager. Just the three of them.

Ever since I was little, I have watched *The Sound of*

Music from start to finish every year. It's one of the all-time classic musicals that will be revered forever in its brilliance, largely because of Julie's voice. That voice was such a sweet sound, scaling four octaves, so pitch-perfect they could tune other voices to it. She conquered Broadway as Queen Guinevere in *Camelot* and appeared in many movies, including Disney's *Mary Poppins*, for which she won an Oscar. She has such variation in talent having written notable children's books and voicing the Queen in the *Shrek* franchise. Julie Andrews is so immeasurably talented, she can do anything as proven by the incredible amount of awards she has won—so many, one couldn't possibly name them all. I was very much looking forward to serving her.

The first thing I noticed was her firm posture, posture that only added to the respect I already had for her. She emits grace and dignity, it oozes from her, it's almost intimidating and I felt as if I was in the presence of royalty. Each of the girls had one doll and only that doll. It was a very quiet flight. The children were amazingly well behaved, and I never heard a loud word the entire time. Their manners were impeccable. I offered them everything I could think of, but they politely refused most of it and were just happy to be left alone. I do not think I have ever been more impressed with a woman traveling with children.

As they were leaving the aircraft to go about their lives, the girls thanked me wholeheartedly for serving them. Thank me? I felt that I should have thanked them for the privilege.

Snap out of it, people! Have you flown on an airline recently? It's not even close to the scene I just described. The kids I see today are rude, self-absorbed, and ill mannered. Julie Andrews said it best when she said: "Some people regard discipline as a chore. For me, it is a kind of order that sets me free to fly."

LIONEL RICHIE

Sometimes, on Regent Air, the action was in the rear of the airplane instead of the bar area. Private staterooms were in the back along with the barber chair and the extra large lavatory. You just never knew what monkey business was going to happen or when.

Most of the other flight attendants didn't like the rear of the plane because it was more work. To make up the beds, you had to ask the occupants to vacate the staterooms. Then you had to recline all four seats and push them together with no "rear side cracks." After you wrestled the seats flat, you had to pull and tug at the custom-fitted sheets (think motor home or bunk bed here), put pillowcases on pillows, and finish with cushy blankets. Once this task was accomplished, your guests could return to sleep or do whatever it is they did in lieu of sleeping. When we began to descend, you had to do it all in reverse. Many times people were not too pleased when you had to roust them into the cabin while you turned the beds back into seats for landing. But I always liked the extra work in the back. After all, what else did I have to do? Besides, the faster the time went by, the sooner I could get to the bar and talk about the wild and crazy flight.

Felicia and I always bid our schedules together so we could devour Manhattan, but also because we had a system working the back of the plane together. She would work on one side and me on the other; if one of us was struggling, the other would help out. The chief pursers always liked having us on their flights because they never had to worry about the staterooms. Felicia and I were a force to be reckoned with. We even knew how many people were in the bathroom and for how long. More than once we had to intervene to get them out because landing was imminent—or if what they were really doing in there became apparent to the rest of the passengers.

On this particular flight, singer Lionel Richie had booked a stateroom and was traveling alone. He was at the peak of his career, flying high with a successful album and the hit single

"All Night Long." Originally, from The Commodores fame, he went solo and onto worldwide fame, mainly notable for some truly ("Truly" being one of his breakout solo hits) incredible love songs. I'm sure there are many rug rats running around who were conceived to his music. Incidentally, he is the adoptive father of reality TV star Nicole Richie, whose godfather was pop singer Michael Jackson.

Felicia was Lionel's flight attendant. It started with our safety demonstration. He would not take his eyes off her. She had his complete attention (Finally, Ha!). He was a blast, very outgoing, and funny. Although he was teasing us both, he was really giving Felicia a hard time. I thought it was all in good humor, because we we're laughing so much and because everyone knew how he adored his beloved wife. I really believed he was just entertaining us with his pursuit of Felicia.

We spent a lot of time in his stateroom because he was enthralled with the whole concept of Regent Air, and Felicia, and because the rest of the plane was in a bad mood. That flight included never-ending thunderstorms that jostled the plane all over the sky. We could barely walk without being thrown about, which only added to the ongoing teasing in the back of the airplane. Lionel Richie was just waiting for Felicia to fall on top of him, which on that flight would not have been a stretch.

Personally, I love turbulence. I get a big kick out of the ups and downs and sideway tossing of turbulent air. I know it's strange, but it always puts me in a good mood. I have been known to do cartwheels down the aisle when there weren't any passengers onboard. It's so much fun doing gymnastics when the plane is doing them with you—or would that be against you?

On this flight, almost everyone was nervous and frightened by the horrendous weather. Turbulence and just plain old flying brings out the wimpy in many. A very wealthy couple here in Southern California always holds hands across the aisle on takeoff. One of the owner's wives would freak when we hit the smallest bumps. I always made her drinks stronger when I was forewarned by the pilots of upcoming turbulence.

Some of the passengers on Lionel's flight were mad because they couldn't get any work done, and some passengers were angry just because it was bumpy. So naturally we hung out with Lionel, who was laughing and joking, thoroughly enjoying himself and seemingly impervious to the airplane being jostled around the sky like a two-year-old's toy. Felicia and I have very outgoing personalities, and we all just seemed to mesh well. By the time we reached New York, we felt like the one and only Lionel Richie was now a good friend and one we looked forward to seeing again. We'd had a ball.

I didn't realize he was in lust with Felicia. I was clueless. I had watched them joking around and one-upping each other. I even noticed that his eyes never veered very far from her. Some of his comments to her were a little more personal and maybe a bit inappropriate, but I didn't pay much attention. I felt like her replies to him were just to keep him on his toes because she has a quick wit.

As we descended he invited us to his home on the East Coast (or some home on the East Coast). That was the first time I'd been invited to a famous person's home. I wanted to go, and I still didn't get it. I was very young, not only chronologically, but in wisdom. Since he was married I thought he just enjoyed the company of two really fun girls—I know, stupid, eh? I had walked or stumbled around that flight like I was someone that Lionel Richie wanted to hang out with. I never conceived the fact that he wanted Felicia until she practically drew me a map. Du-oh! Does that mean we can't go to his house?

After Felicia spelled this out for me at the bar in the hotel, I felt like a dim-witted, idealist of a young woman, and I made my first mental notes: naiveté has no place in this business. No matter how many invitations I might receive in my career, professionalism would take precedence. And that men are pigs.

DEAN MARTIN AND MILTON BERLE

In the middle of winter on a brutally cold and windy night in New York, we briefed for a flight back to Los Angeles. I grabbed a copy of the manifest to see what exciting name might be there and to my sincere delight I saw: Dean Martin.

Dean Martin is my personal higher power. I have always had some sort of attachment to him and I don't really know why. Even now I have his photo right next to my bed. He fascinates me. The famous "Rat Packer" was so laid back, so cool, a crooner with a sultry charm. He was a comic genius, too, especially in the early days with Jerry Lewis. Once when I had a ten-day layover in Milan, his music was playing in every store. I bought his CD mainly for "That's Amore," which played every twenty minutes in Italy!

My parents and I used to cruise in our boat around our lake house and listen to Dean Martin and the rest of the Rat Pack singing and ribbing each other, all off the cuff. It was so

100

entertaining! And so relaxing. Maybe that's why I adored him. He was relaxing, with a mellow, funny twist. When people were late arriving to the plane, I often played videos of his old TV shows, as well as Johnny Carson's, to entertain the ones who were on time.

Dean boarded the plane before all the other passengers. I thought it was so he could avoid all the ogling eyes and maybe because he was a little tipsy. He was traveling with his manager who asked me to be sure to keep everyone out of the stateroom, especially Milton Berle. I took Dean's beverage selection: scotch "neat" with a soda bottle back, no ice. Never, had I served a drink faster.

Milton Berle and his wife were in the two seats directly outside of Dean's stateroom. They were a hoot, and he was as lively and jovial as you would expect "Uncle Miltie" to be. Milton Berle had acquired two nicknames: "Uncle Miltie," because he would sign off on his television shows by telling children to "listen to their Uncle Miltie and go to bed," and "Mr. Television" because he was instrumental in bringing the medium to life and thus selling actual television sets! He was well known for his comedy and—well, ahem—something else.

The first issue with Milton was that of the well-known extension of his left hand: his cigar. Yes, he actually lit one up. I asked him to extinguish it, but he lit it again and again and again. Finally the chief purser threatened to ban him off the airline if he lit it one more time. I was really surprised that he wouldn't just put the darn thing out. Why be such a pain?

I don't think Milton knew Dean was behind him until about halfway through the flight. Milton was wandering around the plane chatting with anyone who would listen. I think he peeked behind Dean's curtain. When I came to the back of the airplane, Milton was in Dean's stateroom. I attempted to intervene. I shoved the curtain aside and was about to scold him, but before I could say anything, he looked at me and said, "Do you know that I have the biggest schlong you have ever seen?" I thought to my young and unworldly self, *Is a schlong what I think it is?* I told Milton to scoot, but he wasn't listening. I had to enlist Felicia to help me get Milton out of Dean's stateroom. The bizarre problems of flying the rich and famous!

Felicia and I pushed the curtain aside again—just as Milton dropped his pants! Yep, dropped his pants and his skivvies so everything was hanging out. I was shocked! Felicia, however, remained cool and said, "Seen one, seen 'em all!" And with that she shoved me out of the stateroom because I was dumbstruck and turning thirteen shades of red. Then, laughing the whole time, she ushered out Milton, who zipped up his pants and waltzed back to his wife. Let me just answer the question that you all are thinking right now: yes, it was huge.

As that little bit of gossip circulated, everyone began to suspect that Dean Martin was indeed on the airplane. Now Felicia and I really had our work cut out for us, so we flat out lied: "No, Dean Martin is not on the plane, Milton is just goofing around." It sort of worked, except for the people who decided they had to use the restroom every fifteen minutes so they could loiter around the staterooms. We busted them too, telling them they couldn't block the aisle or that the seatbelt sign was on or whatever.

By the end of the flight, after all the other passengers had deplaned, Dean Martin had to be carried out on a stair chair—he was just too drunk to walk. I have read that Dean only drank apple juice on stage with the Rat Pack, that he only began to drink scotch after his son died. But I have also read he drank scotch on stage. Who really knows? It was a sad way to say goodbye, but at least I got to meet him.

ROGER PENSKE

I was asked if I could fly an extended Pacific Rim trip for Roger Penske, a major player in the car-racing world. Roger has been involved in every aspect of car racing from NASCAR to

Formula One, but at this time, he was famous for the Indy circuit

with his Marlboro cars and drivers winning races right and left.

In fact, Roger Penske owns the most successful Indy car racing

team to date. He is now chairman of the Penske Corporation,

which owns several business entities, including Penske

Automotive Group with over 300 car dealerships, Penske Racing

and Penske Truck Leasing. His revenues exceed 1.1 billion and

he employs over 36,000 people worldwide.

We were leaving from Long Beach, California, and I was

very excited, as it would be my first time to places like Taiwan (I

saw a huge silk batik of an Asian elephant hanging behind the

counter in a small shop in Taiwan and refused to leave without

it) and Singapore. I had flown Roger Penske on another

company's jet and knew he was a dear man. In fact, the planet

would be far better off if more men were like Roger Penske.

When traveling overseas, an experienced flight attendant

will prepare for the unexpected, so I purchased a variety of items, just in case, along with my usual list of staples. Because I am such a fan of Asia and always impatient to get there—this is just idiotic -I arrived at the airport way before my "show" time and began to prepare the galley and cabin.

As I looked about I felt something was missing, but could not put my finger on it, so I just kept working. I put things in their places and arranged the flowers, but all of the sudden it hit me: Oh no! I left all the perishables in my refrigerator at home! Panic! Panic! Panic! Ok, wait, slow down, and take a deep breath. What are you going to do? You stupid, blonde moron. What an idiot! At that point my heart felt like it was going to jump out of my chest and flop around on the floor. Panic! Panic! Panic! Take another deep breath or you're going to pass out.

All right, let's see, you've got to go back and get it, you just don't have a choice, and fortunately you're really early. Maybe not so idiotic, after all. All right then, where's my car? Crap! They've already parked it! (Some of the FBOs are so nice to the flight attendants and pilots that after we've unloaded our luggage and supplies, the rampers will park our cars inside the hangar so we have clean vehicles upon our return—the perks of flying the rich and famous!

Okay, then I have to take a car from the FBO. Oh no, there's going (there is always traffic on this particular section of freeway!) to be traffic. Ok, I have to use the carpool lane, but I'll need another person. Wait, remember Julio, the janitor? Get him! Ok, I see the manager over there. I'll get a car from him, grab Julio on my way out and hit the carpool lane. That is my only option.

I screamed my problem to the ground manager, got the keys to a crew car (cars that the FBOs let flight crew borrow in lieu of renting), grabbed a frightened Julio (I actually grabbed the mop out of his hand and stuck it in the bucket) and drove like a maniac back to Newport Beach only to realize the keys to my house were on my key ring in my car in the hangar! I should just shoot myself now and forget about it.

I prayed like no one has ever prayed before that I had left the kitchen window open a tiny bit like I usually do. Then again, if I was a smart chick (and clearly I'm not), I would have closed the window before I left on a twelve-day trip. Please let me have forgotten to close the window. When I turned the corner to my house I immediately looked up at my kitchen window—and it was cracked open! This smart/stupid, stupid/smart gig was really stressing me out. After I shimmied through the kitchen window and retrieved the groceries, I came out the front door and noticed the expression on Julio's face: he looked like he was in a horror flick. Julio didn't speak much English, and I don't think he knew where he was going or why. My speed-demon driving probably scared the pants off him, not to mention watching me breaking and entering. We made it back to the hangar uneventfully (although, Julio almost broke his leg trying to get out of the car , literally getting his leg caught in the seat belt) and I began to put

108

the rest of the groceries away. With all that I had been through, I was still ready over an hour early.

Our first stop was Anchorage, Alaska for fuel and to change pilots, but I stayed with the plane. You couldn't have torn me out anyway, no way. Roger Penske was just as he had been before: very gracious and polite—like the sweet neighbor kid who lived next door when you were growing up, except this guy is smart, exceptionally intelligent with a never-ending zest for life, and a ginormous bank account. He used the plane like a hotel. We flew at night while he slept, and when we arrived in a new city, he was ready to conquer the world, or at least the Pacific part of the world.

One of the countries we visited was Jakarta, Indonesia. On the drive from the airport to the hotel, I saw overwhelming poverty. There were dilapidated buildings, rundown shacks and people loitering about everywhere, especially children. But when we arrived at the hotel, everything changed.

109

In Asia, there is a keycard box inside your room. Put the card in and the power turns on; remove it and it turns off. You cannot waste electricity. When I put my keycard in the box, the drapes slowly opened outward, the stereo came on low, the lights came on dim, and the television came on with no sound. It was late at night and I was perplexed. Gradually, I became mesmerized by my surroundings. The room was glowing with ambience; there was a huge bathtub to my right and a separate shower to my left. I was standing in the middle of an enormous bathroom, yet I hadn't entered the bedroom. It was a long elevator ride up, but I wasn't expecting such a view. It was magnificent, a spectacular surprise and an awe-inspiring moment never to be repeated. I ordered a glass of wine from room service, sat at the desk and wrote myself a note reminding myself why I do this, forsaking my family and personal life. When we finally made our way to the Gold Coast of Australia, Mr. Penske was off to the Australian Grand Prix and the pilots and me to our hotel. Thirty minutes after I walked into my hotel room, there was a knock on my door. It was a special delivery—Roger Penske had given each of us full credentials to the race! We watched it from his suite directly over the track, all the while schmoozing with his friends and colleagues. When we wandered down into the pits, he immediately acknowledged us and introduced us to all kinds of people, and we sort of hung out with him. We had a blast, and it was an outstanding day.

On our return flight to Long Beach we had to stop for fuel in Pago Pago, American Samoa. As we began our approach, the beauty of the island became clear. The forest green of the rising volcano contrasts with the flat, incredibly white sand beaches and bright blue, crystal clear ocean. The runway was parallel to the ocean and it looked as if the waves were going to lap up and over it. I would have loved to spend the night and explore the island, but all we did was get off and walk around to stretch our legs. Someday I intend to go back.

Once in the air again, I adjusted all the seats to make sleeping berths for my four passengers. That left nowhere for me to sit or sleep, except my jump seat, which is very uncomfortable for sleeping. Eventually, I rearranged all the briefcases in the forward closet, took the coats off of the hangers, padded them around the brief cases and sat down. I was out. I slept, as did my four passengers, almost the entire way to Honolulu. It had been a long trip and everyone was exhausted. When I awoke, I had to pry my butt off the briefcases; somehow it had adhered. Awaiting us in Honolulu were two fresh pilots because the others were dead tired and in need of a long rest.

I had been home about a week from this trip when there was a knock on my front door. I opened it and was greeted by another special delivery. This one was a huge box with an envelope from Roger Penske. He had written a letter to me and the pilots complimenting our service, timeliness, courtesy, and professionalism. The box itself contained all kinds of "Penske" mementos—sweatshirts, t-shirts, jackets, and hats. See, I told you he was a great guy. Nice guys finish first.

DIONNE WARWICK

On another cross-country trip, I was fortunate enough to have pop singer Dionne Warwick on my flight. She was the sweetest, most down-to-earth famous woman I had yet to meet.

Dionne Warwick is probably best known for collaborating with composer Burt Bacharach on classic songs like "Do You Know the Way to San Jose?" and "I'll Never Fall in Love Again." And perhaps you all know she is Whitney Houston's cousin. She later did a stint on Donald Trump's television show *Celebrity Apprentice*, but seemed quite different from the woman I'd met years earlier.

I thought she was lovely. She asked me questions about everything and was genuinely interested in my answers and my life. A lot of celebrities are all about themselves, but not Dionne

Warwick. She had me talking about myself most of the time. (To be fair, I usually don't have a problem with this.) I don't know why she cared about me, but she did. By the time we landed in New York, I knew nothing about her, yet she knew everything about me. I think she might have outsmarted me!

When she asked me what my plans were for the layover, I told her I was going shopping at Bloomingdales. I had yet to cruise through that shopping Mecca and was eager to see what all the hoopla was about. Her animated response was about how blooming awesome Bloomies was. Then she asked if I wouldn't mind picking something up for her. Well, of course I wouldn't! I would be delighted to be Dionne Warwick's personal shopper! I didn't know it but Bloomingdales had underwear with the word "Bloomies" embellished across the butt. Apparently they were quite popular at the time, and Dionne wanted some. So I set off to explore Bloomingdales, bought myself things I couldn't afford and her blooming underwear.

When she arrived at the aircraft for the return flight, she was wearing the most elegant full-length mink coat. Feeling like she and I were pals by now, I asked Ms. Warwick if I could try it on. She not only allowed that, but insisted I wear it. "I can wear your mink? Because, you know I will." And wear it I did—the entire flight. Okay, except for the meal service—I had to take it off for that. It would have really sucked, if I had spilled salad dressing on her mink coat.

Actually this coat was far better off on me than hung safely in the closet. In winter, every person had at least one coat, and there simply was not enough room for them. There were times when we jam-packed so many $20,000 mink coats in the closet, hangers were not required—they held themselves up. Some celebrities even traveled with more than one, like heaven forbid they should be seen in the same coat twice. There had to have been days when the rear closet was worth more than the airplane itself! When this happened, any unused space was game for coat hanging. I wonder what the Federal Aviation Authority would have said if they discovered that I lined the life rafts with coats? Well, if you're gonna ditch an airplane…

When I gave Ms. Warwick the bag with the "Bloomies" underwear, she took out half and gave them to me! I loved those underwear. I wore them with huge amounts of self-importance because, after all, Dionne Warwick had bought them for me. I wore them until they turned into thongs, and then into dental floss, actually, I have one on right now…

DIANA ROSS

At one point in my career, I was flying to New York and back to Los Angeles on the same day, otherwise known as "turns." These are brutally long days, and it can be difficult not to get cranky, crabby, or impatient on the return to LA, but the return trips were always the best flights because the workday was over for the passengers, and they were ready to party.

One morning while getting ready for another lengthy date with the sky I was disappointed because they were no "good" names on my manifest. I had become spoiled by now as I had flown with so many celebrities—most of my flights included at least one famous or well-to-do person of interest. I would scan the manifest to see who was seated where, in case I had to prepare to battle over serving my favorite celebrity or football hero or Wall Street icon. So, on this rather dull morning I wasn't all that excited about working a fourteen-hour day in 2 percent humidity.

Just before closing the main cabin door, a late arrival came slowly up the stairs—Diana Ross. Diana Ross, one of the "Supremes" and a soul legend, a Motown mogul, probably best known for an amazing song, "Ain't No Mountain High Enough." Diana Ross glided across the airplane in this bright outfit with a cape-like jacket that billowed and flowed behind her. The ensemble of yellow and green was vibrant and vivid, almost glowing with a chartreuse blaze. Her hair was big, huge actually—all black and frizzy. Because of the static onboard the airplane her hair really stood up, it was four times the size of her head. Remember the eighties? Everything was big: hair, earrings, shoulder pads, marijuana joints and lines of cocaine!

She sashayed onboard like she was someone, who of course she was and reeked of the perfume of the decade: Giorgio. She must have sprayed her whole outfit, because that airplane smelled like Giorgio all the way to New York and back to LA. A pet-peeve of mine: if you are going to be in an enclosed space, do not apply excessive amounts of cologne or perfume and asphyxiate the rest of us! Some of you need to learn this right now.

Ross was unapproachable. I believe she felt superior to everyone else. Graciousness was almost nonexistent. She would not look me in the eye (another pet peeve of mine) and ordered us around like we were her servants. She was impatient and rude which made her ugly and unattractive to me. She would have made an outstanding Wicked Witch of the West.

When I first began to wait on the rich and famous, this kind of behavior would make me try harder. As I became savvier, however, I would remind myself that someone else's behavior was about them, not me.

DON KING

Don King, the notorious boxing promoter, chartered the airplane to attend a boxing match in the Niagara Falls area. He had a wild reputation. He's been sued many times, and he's relentlessly the butt of many a comedy sketch or cartoon villain. You'd think he was a total "strong arm" kind of guy, but he was nothing like that with me. I had a great time during his charter.

When he climbed the stairs and boarded the plane, he was so big and tall that his hair went straight up to the top of the headliner. As he walked through the cabin, his hair touched the top of the airplane and bent backwards like an upside-down "L" or the number "7" or better yet, like the way bumper cars attach at the top of the ride! My goodness, this was such an amusing sight, watching him walk through the cabin while his hair followed behind. I started giggling and grinning because it was just so funny looking. Silly really, but it was to set the tone for the rest of the trip.

Don King came onboard with his entourage and some boxers I didn't know, but that the pilots were all keyed up about. He was a chipper fellow, very outgoing and gregarious. He reminded me of a black Santa Claus! He was definitely in his element, telling everyone where to sit and what to do, like the director of his own personal play, which I guess is what he does. After we had taken off and reached our cruising altitude, he began to wander around and chitchat with the crew. He asked all about the airplane and about each of us, and then he asked us if we would pose for a photo. We took turns sitting on the couch with him, laughing and taking pictures and being captivated by his energy and enthusiasm. Then he went up to the cockpit, where he stayed for a long while. I'm sure he was entertaining the pilots and suffering through (what an oxymoron!) their admiration of him and interest in boxing!

Don King invited the crew to a party that night and the boxing match the next day. The party was in a huge banquet room inside a remarkably fancy hotel. Everywhere you looked there were massive spreads of food next to elaborate ice sculptures and enormous flowing champagne glass fountains. The room was decorated in all white with gold-covered chairs, white tablecloths with gold runners and napkins, and glitter strewn about. Looming over all this was a gigantic crystal chandelier. The effect was ostentatious, to be sure.

As I took in the scene, I was struck by the contrast of the pale white and shiny gold décor in the midst of a sea of black—black people, I mean. With the exception of the flight crew—we were some of the only white people in the room.

Then something unbelievable happened. We were eating and drinking and having a groovy old time, when Don King came up to us and addressed us by our first names! With all he had going on, he remembered our names. It seems my dad was right: remembering someone's name is powerful.

As we were departing for our return to LA, the pilots told us that we would be flying over Niagara Falls at an extremely low altitude. Apparently, Don King had thrown his weight around and had somehow managed what the pilots thought was an impossible feat: getting clearance to fly over this unique wonder of the world relatively low in the sky.

When we reached the Falls, you could have heard a pin drop on that airplane—a coup in itself, especially with that crowd. No one spoke. No one wanted to ruin the moment of beauty and splendor below. It was such an extraordinary and unforgettable opportunity. Not to mention the sight of rear ends lined up butt-to-butt to gaze out the windows. "Only in America, folks"—a famous Don King quip!

On a side note, I also had the opportunity to get clearance to fly over the rim of the Grand Canyon. It became a restricted airspace after sightseeing planes kept crashing into each other, but somehow at that time we were allowed to fly just above it. It was spectacular! Everything looks more formidable from above.

During this trip we landed in Page, Arizona so the passengers could take a boat tour of Lake Powell. Page, Arizona is on Indian reservations time, meaning they observe Daylight Savings time. The rest of the state of Arizona does not. They are the only state in the nation that does not change their clocks- due to weather.

They are not the only places that don't change time. Some counties do it in various states. It is very embarrassing when the passengers ask you what time you are landing and the pilots give me the wrong answer! But, it has happened a few times. Or like when Hugo Chavez changed the country of Venezuela's time zone just because he could! I learned to listen to the people on the ground—they know. Ah, but I digress.

Now let's shift gears.

LARRY FLYNT

One beautiful morning when I was just about to enjoy a lengthy bike ride, I received an urgent call to get to the airport as soon as possible. Screech, change gears, and put bike away. Throw more clothes in an already packed suitcase (chronically conscientious), struggle into my uniform and haul ass to the airport.

In 1983, Larry Flynt was running for president of the United States and had chartered the plane to hit the campaign trail. A "Larry Flynt for President" campaign ad went: "Good morning, I am your worst nightmare come true: a fabulously wealthy pornographer with the courage and willingness to spend

124

my last dime to expose how you are perverting the Constitution of this great land. Now let's get down to business."

Larry Flynt, publisher of *Hustler*, was the first pornographer to show, ahem, well, let's just say "more detailed parts" of a woman's body inside the pages of his magazine. A few years prior to his candidacy, he was shot in an assassination attempt that left him partially paralyzed and wheelchair-bound for the rest of his life.

He was brought up the stairs to the airplane in a stair chair, also known as "straight backs," in an air of seriousness. He had more security than entourage, but I suppose after what he'd been through, one might be on the skittish side. All the security detail had guns—lots of guns—and the pilots took issue (go figure, huh). It took a long time, but eventually Larry Flynt, his security and mine - the pilots, finally reached an agreement about the guns. Let me just say, if hair was to set the tone for Don King's charter, guns were to set the tone for Larry Flynt's.

Once we were airborne, Flynt had porn showing on every television screen (there were several television's on Regent Air). Then he asked us to put on his T-shirts: "Larry Flynt for President." The very next thing he asked was if we would sit in his lap on his wheelchair and take pictures with him. This photo session did not have the same connotation as Don King's. There was no laughter and no fun involved. It was quite the opposite. The air was tense. I felt awkward and uncomfortable, almost violated just by sitting on this guy's lap.

There were strange activities going on in the staterooms too, but because of my tender age and unwillingness to go back there, I stayed in the front part of the cabin. I heard stories from the other flight attendants that I wanted no part of.

We traveled around the United States while he campaigned and as much as I love my job, I couldn't wait for this charter to end. I felt I matured ten years flying with Larry Flynt and lost an abundance of innocence that had no place in

126

this environment anyway. Welcome to the real world, baby.

DICK CLARK

When I was flying for Regent Air, flight attendants bid on schedules, just like the airlines do. Normally, we'd spend one night in Newark and return to Los Angeles around the same time the following day. But when we left on a Friday, we had two nights and the whole of Saturday to enjoy the city, so this was the flight I always bid. Many times I'd have the same passengers on both flights going to and from NYC for the weekend.

One Friday night, I was driving to Los Angeles International Airport (LAX) for my usual Friday thru Sunday stint, and wondering what shenanigans might lie ahead because almost every flight or layover had some kind of craziness going on. When I got to our terminal, I immediately grabbed my manifest and saw that Dick Clark was in one of my staterooms, traveling with his father.

127

Dick Clark! "America's Oldest Teenager!" Right on! Barely out of my own teens, I was thoroughly excited to be flying with this icon. Everyone has watched New Years Rockin' Eve with Dick Clark at least once—you know, that one year when you stayed home ! He hosted that show through 2012, the year he passed away. I grew up with his TV show *American Bandstand*.

All the crew hurried about getting the plane ready for our flight, but everyone seemed to be working faster than usual. What none of us realized is that we were all doing it for the same reason: so we wouldn't miss his arrival. Even the office staff was out in force anticipating his appearance. Everyone wanted to shake his hand, the pilots, the ground crew, everyone.

Dick Clark had a line of airline paparazzi waiting for him. In fact, it took him forever to board the aircraft because he stopped to shake everyone's hand. When he finally entered the cabin, a few of the flight attendants and I broke into song, "Start spreading the news, we're leaving today. I want to be a part of it, New York, New York." I began to kick my legs like a Rockette and the other flight attendants followed suit. We had a mini singing, dancing welcome party for Dick Clark and he loved it! So did everyone else; the whole plane was singing. It was truly a moment because he was the absolutely perfect person to perform that song for and yet it was totally off the cuff. We pulled off the ultimate improv that night and it was an ideal way to launch our journey across the continent.

Dick Clark was fabulous, very mellow, kind, and considerate, a wise man that seemed to me to be very peaceful. His father must have been in his eighties or older; he was extremely frail and moved very slowly, sort of shuffling along to get to his seat. With a serene smile on his face, Dick Clark was right beside him, very patient with obvious love, attention, and dedication—the ultimate respect for his father.

I had always wondered why New York was labeled "The

Big Apple." I was sure Dick Clark would be the perfect person to tell me. So I asked him! He thought about it and started to say something, then stopped, took a deep breath, exhaled and sort of mumbled, "I really don't know why." He had this rather bewildered expression on his face and kept looking at me as if he was thinking, "What the heck, why don't I know?" He was definitely puzzled and was at a loss as to why he didn't know. He was returning with us on the Sunday night flight back to LA, so he assured me he would find out because he was curious as well, very curious indeed.

When he reappeared for the flight back to LA, he was beaming at me with the look of "*I know something you want to know!*" Naturally, he had found the answer. It had something to do with an apple being a symbol for freedom. When you took a bite of an apple, you were taking a bite of freedom. So in old Europe, they would relate America to freedom and an apple to New York (Ellis Island being the gateway to freedom). He explained this with great pride and enthusiasm.

I believed this to be true for years, but have since been told that it's not that at all. Apparently, it all started from horse racing in the 1920s. The prizes won for the races were compared to apples. New York, having the ultimate racetrack, had the ultimate prize and therefore "The Big Apple." Okay, before you all start shouting at me—who really knows? In any case, this is what I learned from the time I got to spend with Dick Clark: the world should be about others, not yourself.

LOS ANGELES KINGS

While flying private jets, I was building my repertoire of flight departments that would request me and trying to prove my worthiness to anyone who would take notice. I was then given the opportunity to do something different.

Bruce McNall owned the Los Angeles Kings. Bruce McNall claimed he made his money in coin collection; he eventually went to prison having plead guilty to five counts of conspiracy and fraud—he also defaulted on something in excess of $200 million in bank loans. He was also an airplane enthusiast and owned a personal airplane, a JetStar (Tail#199LA). The LA Kings were doing very well that year, so he bought an older Boeing 727 (Tail # 299LA) and asked my flight attendant broker to help him configure it for the transport of the LA Kings to and from Canada for their hockey games. She in turn asked me and two others to be the flight attendants with her.

We determined what the crew needed, what the players needed, what the owners and coaches needed, and went to work preparing the aircraft. We organized the galley and what our meal service would entail, evaluated safety equipment and adjusted accordingly, tackled a never-ending shopping list, acquired caterers in every city, and scrubbed every inch of that plane. Then we stocked and decorated the cabin with every piece of LA Kings paraphernalia we could find. We put our heart and

132

souls into making that aircraft ready to transport the athletes, the managers, the coaches, the doctors, the dentists, the press, and whoever else might show up.

And we had a system. We would leave Van Nuys airport in Southern California in the early afternoon to be in Canada for game time, and often we would return to Van Nuys after the game. If this was the case, the players would be starving, like they-hadn't-eaten-in-a-week starving. We couldn't feed them fast enough, so it didn't take us long to figure out that we also needed snack baskets of candy, nuts, and cookies in between each two-seat section to hold them over until we got to a level attitude (attitude: when the plane flies straight, but I know what you were thinking) where we could then serve a huge, delicious dinner. My co-worker Stephen (of Liz Taylor story – who we hid in the galley) had the galley all prearranged with individual casserole dishes that the caterers would have filled, usually with lasagna or something of that nature. We three girls would serve the salads, bread, and butter while he was heating up the entrées.

We had two giant ice chests belted in the last row. One was full of beer, soda, and water and the other held Haagen Dazs ice cream bars. By the time those boys got to the airplane, not only were they famished, but parched. They could down a beer or soda in thirty seconds and a single can was rarely enough. Eventually I learned to just stand in the back of the cabin and chuck cans to the players as they boarded—beer if they won - soda if they lost.

McNall had a rule: if they won, the players could drink alcohol, and if they lost, then no. I understood that well enough but it was difficult if the team lost because this rule didn't apply to the entire plane. The front of the plane (like first class but the seats were the same) was designated seating for management and doctors, press, and the like. The back of the airplane was for the players. The galley and bulkheads separated the two sections. I had a hard time with the players not being able to drink in the back when the front was having a good ol' time, and especially when Wayne Gretsky was up there drinking with them. *Uh, isn't this a team sport? Oh, and aren't you a coach? Maybe you screwed up?* I always felt sorry for the players. After all, they were the ones out there getting their teeth bashed in and sweating and bleeding all over the back of the airplane. If they couldn't drink, the others should at least show some respect. Or, I could take matters into my own hands and sneak wine from the front of the plane and give it to the players who pled with me.

The players would have showered and changed but they would not have had time to address all their injuries before boarding. Many of them would strip down to their undies in order to ice up all their hard-hit body parts or abrasions. There were many times when I would giggle to myself, thinking that no one would believe I was flying across the United States with a bunch of charming naked men begging for alcohol (again, the problems of flying the rich and famous!).

Our star player was "The Great One," Wayne Gretsky. In 1988, Bruce McNall engineered a purchase of him for a whopping fifteen million dollars (an unheard of amount at the time) from the Edmonton Oilers (who we would come head to head with over and over again), along with Gretsky's good pals, Marty McSorly and Mike Krushelnyski. Wayne Gretsky always said he would come only if McSorly and Kruschelnyski came with him, but I'm not sure he had a vote in the matter or what the truth was. All I know is the entire country of Canada was mourning the loss of their national treasure. And they were pissed at us for taking him.

I have read this trade was institutional in bringing hockey to the forefront of otherwise ignorant fans and changing the future of all of hockey competition in the Northern Hemisphere. It certainly shook the ignorance out of me. And it must have had some indirect responsibility for the rise of the San Jose Sharks, the Mighty Ducks of Anaheim, and probably others as well.

Apparently Wayne Gretsky was afraid of flying. The pilots on the JetStar told us they were taking Gretsky with them for the next flight instead of him traveling on the 727 with the rest of us. The JetStar pilots wanted to put Gretsky in the jump seat between the two of them and explain how an airplane flies - the theory being that understanding would relieve his anxiety. It must work, because we never heard anything about his fear of flying after that. Or maybe they made this up so Gretsky could fly in the JetStar?

All the players were adorable, but I was totally enamored with Marty McSorly. He was also a fan favorite and came to the Kings with the label "Gretsky's Bodyguard." McSorly was the rebel, the fighter, the one always in the penalty box; he made hockey interesting. He had Gretsky's back and my attention. He always sat with Steve Duchesne (who would go on to win the Stanley Cup during his final season). I called Duchesne "Douchebag" and McSorly "McSourly." They would sleep with their heads propped up against each other, with a pillow in between—it was just too cute.

Our goalie, Kelly Hrudey—what a sweetheart—seemed too nice and reserved to be a hockey player, but he was much more than that. He was an unbelievable hockey-puck-stopping-goalie-guru. He was instrumental in the Kings progressing into the division playoffs, as I suppose they all were. And it was hard not to drool over Luc Robitaille. He was so appealing, especially when almost naked. (He holds the title of Stanley Cup winner 2012 as President of Business Operations for the LA Kings.) Then there was Rob Blake and Tony Granato, I mean the list goes on and on. I adored each and every one of them.

After that season it was time for the Kings to go to spring training in Calgary. We stayed at the Banff Springs Hotel, which was built in 1888 and designed after a Scottish castle. It definitely looks the part. The exterior is dark brick covered in moss with turrets everywhere, resembling what you might picture while reading a period novel. The interior is a maze. The players were assigned their own floor of rooms, the crew another and so on. The players were forbidden from our floor and the bars and disco. The crew hung out in the disco. When I mentioned this to "McSourly" at a game in Calgary, he decided to sneak into the disco the next night. He and I were dancing up a storm when he got caught. He was fined for his behavior, but as the rebel of the clan, I don't think he much cared.

One night on the way to the game in Calgary, which was about an hour and a half from the hotel, the pilots decided to go on the bus with the players instead of in the van with the flight attendants. That night it was just us three girls and our male co-worker in this huge van they'd given us for our transportation and shopping needs.

We went to the game dressed in all our Kings attire. We were walking, talking, real-life advertisements for the LA Kings. Every part of our bodies that could be clothed, was clothed with

LA KINGS. McNall had changed the LA Kings colors from purple/gold to black/silver to coincide with the LA Raiders that played just up the way at The Coliseum. (At the time, the Kings played at the Great Forum; the Staples Center hadn't been built yet.) We definitely stuck out in our black/white/silver garb when everyone else was in red and yellow. Canada, being the ungracious hosts they were, sat us way up in the top of the venue. What was overlooked on their part, however, was hilarious. The Calgary Flames' mascot was a giant red and yellow stuffed flame. He stood right in front of us and totally blocked our view, all while mercilessly taunting us. But, since the huge flame was such an eyesore, he created a ruckus and therefore we ended up getting a great amount of attention and our own free publicity, despite their trying to conceal us in the nosebleed section!

Heading back to the hotel after this game, it started snowing and the road became icy. I was driving like I always did. I learned to drive our motor home when I was all of twelve.

My father taught me how to drive in the snow and ice and how to

navigate maps, so I never trusted any other flight attendant

behind the wheel—especially in New York where if you weren't

aggressive, you were road kill. I sat a person over each wheel

well to create some traction, but we were still slipping and

sliding all over the place. We passed all kinds of cars that had

skidded off the road into ditches. It took us forever to get back to

the hotel, but we made it. The next day I heard that the bus with

the players took hours longer than we did!

I am an avid snow skier and have been blessed with many

opportunities to ski all around the world. So while on layover in

Banff, I took it upon myself to ski Lake Louise Mountain. Since

I believed myself to be such an accomplished skier, I decided to

go straight to the top of the mountain. That's all fine and dandy,

except for, well, I was in Canada! I never took into consideration

that there were not many people on the chairlift, or that I may not

be skilled enough to ski ice—a solid sheet of ice, a steep,

unforgiving ice mountain. I got off the chairlift and was basically alone on top of what looked like a dooming glacier. I was freezing and really had no other option than to ski down, but that proved impossible. I ended up taking off my skis, putting them sideways across my lap as I slid down on my ass. I always felt like that was Canada getting even!

Sidebar, skiing around the world can be very interesting. While skiing in Austria once, I discovered that they played classic American Disco in EVERY bar on the slopes. And there was always a tree trunk with a hammer and a box of nails, either in the bar or directly outside the front door. Apparently, so you can see how drunk you are if you can't hit the nail into the tree trunk. But I can't do that sober, so not sure how that worked! It was fun though!

Anyway, as the season progressed, the LA Kings made it into the playoffs. That was the challenging part of flying for a sports team. You never knew if you were working the next day until the game you were watching was over. If the game went into overtime, you were really screwed. You couldn't go to bed until you knew if you had to get up. You couldn't plan anything because you never knew what you were doing ahead of time.

My boyfriend was always very tolerant of my wacky schedule, but when the Kings' games began to dictate my life, and, therefore, his, his patience began to wear thin. Trying to make up for it, I brought home one of the player's hockey sticks. I told him that it was Kelly Hrudey's goalie stick because he was a huge fan. I even signed Kelly Hrudey's name on it, so it looked as if he had autographed it. I only made one mistake: goalie sticks are different than the other players' and I had just taken the first stick I saw. One would think that as much as I learned about hockey, as educated as I became, as knowledgeable of all the rules I learned, I would have, at the very least, at the very minimum, learned *that*.

LOS ANGELES LAKERS

143

Though the LA Kings lost in the playoffs, it had been one of their best seasons to date. I was in dire need of some time off, but then I received a phone call: "Will you work the 727 again for the Lakers basketball playoffs?"

"Why, yes. Yes, I will."

Bruce McNall loaned the plane out to the Los Angeles Lakers basketball organization. It was more fun than work flying the Kings: the Lakers should be a gas, I thought.

Less than twenty-four hours later, I received another call, could I do a seven-day charter to the Caribbean?

That's one flight to the Caribbean, sit for five days and return. "Oh man. Well, of course, I want to." I tried to beg off the Lakers' gig, but I couldn't get out of it. It's the nature of this business, and the old Golden Rule to do unto others and all that. So, I flew the Lakers.

At the time, they were in the playoffs with the Phoenix

Suns. After our first flight we very quickly realized that changes were going to have to be made. The players just didn't fit well in the plane. Legs, arms, and enormous hands were everywhere and I constantly tripped over their humongous, giganotosaurus feet. I actually fell over Vlade Divac's shoes and landed on top of him. He said something to me in his broken English, but I have no idea what; I never could understand him.

After much discussion, we eventually came to the conclusion that we had to find a way to accommodate the bottom half of their bodies. We accomplished that by taking out every other row of seats, which gave them ample legroom and kept most of their feet out of the aisles. It worked, although I still tripped over size 22 shoes occasionally. Seriously, size 22! Can you imagine?

Because we only had a forty-five minute flight, there was no meal service, just snacks and beverages. What I found amazing was that the players would drain a soda in one swallow—just one swallow! Again we made adjustments, and served two of everything they asked for. Which slightly worked, although they were still mass-consuming men, kind of like the "Coneheads" on *Saturday Night Live*. I guess that's why they get paid so well, their food and drink habits must cost a bloody fortune.

MICHAEL MILKEN

One of my first flights on a private jet was on a brand new Gulfstream IV. The majority of private jets in Southern California are located in either Van Nuys or Burbank airports, certainly for convenience to Hollywood, the television studios, and the greater surrounding Los Angeles area. There are some at LAX, but not many because this airport is too large and too busy to be suitable; although, I have repositioned there many, many times to pick up passengers coming in on international flights.

Michael Milken had a beautiful airplane and a gorgeous hangar to house it in at Van Nuys airport. This hangar was the nicest I had been in (I'm talking millions of dollars nice), even though it was basically an airplane garage with office space. The aircraft was equally as stunning, all white and pale grey leather, very clean and serene looking. It was very neat and tidy and an easy airplane to work, even though I had no idea what I was doing at that time. In those days nobody trained you; it was sort of sink or swim.

I had never heard of Michael Milken and knew nothing about him. All I was concerned with was getting my first private flight over with. I wasn't confident in my ability to prepare the food correctly or serve him without ignoring him too much or bugging the crap out of him. I was dreadfully nervous, but I didn't need to be. He was the coolest guy. I don't know if he sensed my apprehension, but he immediately put me at ease. He was very polite and well mannered, relaxed, and cheery.

Milken later became known as the "Junk Bond King" and was indicted for racketeering and securities fraud. He paid more than $1 billion in fines and spent time in prison. I don't know a lot about all the junk bond issue, but I suppose if you're being sneaky and making an exorbitant amount of money doing it, then you don't have any right to be in a bad mood.

We flew to Teterboro, New Jersey, which is where almost all private jets land in order to get to Manhattan. There is simply no room at Kennedy, La Guardia, or Newark airports, and you need time slots (a window of time where your arrival is expected) to land. Even if you get in, you could easily be parked in the "north forty," a van ride away from the FBO, which is problematic for a number of reasons. Plus, if you're late for your time slot, forget about it.

When we arrived in Teterboro, I was very relieved I had conquered the first-flight jitters. I managed to stumble through the trip without any major catastrophes. It was, in fact, very smooth, and I quite enjoyed myself. I had served teriyaki chicken skewers over rice, which is hard to screw up, although I didn't know that at the time, plus I only had two passengers and the two pilots. Mr. Milken thanked me profusely and said he was delighted with my service and would look forward to our next flight together. He and I both!

After the passengers departed, we were to dead head (to reposition aircraft with no passengers onboard) to Washington, D.C. We were given an unbelievable departure routing right over the New York skyline. The view was incredible. I had never seen New York from such an angle and the sight of all the towers and bridges was breathtaking. I put a favorite CD on the stereo and was singing along and thinking, *Wow!* I am so lucky. No one could possibly understand what I'm feeling right now. It was so perfect, so unique, and so surreal. I couldn't believe that I had accomplished and even surpassed my dream. Even today, this memory gives me goose bumps; and it's a unique memory because very few people can relate to such an experience.

As we were descending into DC, the sun was setting and

creating a striking backdrop. There I was with the unreal opportunity to see the monuments and capital city in all its grandeur from such an unusual vantage point. Thus began my first sightseeing expedition into our nation's capital. We only had one night in DC, but I made the most of it, arising early the next day to get to the Vietnam Memorial, the Lincoln Memorial, and Washington Monument.

We departed that evening for our return flight. I served a meal that was a little more risky, pulled it off and gained some much needed confidence. Mr. Milken and I had a very nice little chat on the way back, mainly about me, which I thought was considerate. I found him easy to talk to, personable, quick, and sharp. I discovered I rather liked this Michael Milken character. I never saw him again, but I can certainly understand why people get "taken" by these types of men.

AN IPO FLIGHT

While I was still breaking into flying private jets, I had

150

some experience but needed to build a larger repertoire of flight departments in order to make a decent living. I received a call for a charter out of Houston, Texas. We were to deadhead the airplane from Van Nuys to Houston in order to reposition. I had no idea who my passengers were or where exactly we were going. Another unknown journey lay ahead and I was very much looking forward to it.

This charter turned out to be an IPO (initial public offering) flight. I did not know what to expect, but after this excursion, I jumped at the opportunity to fly IPOs in the future. The passengers were keyed up in anticipation of all the money they were going to make—they were truly happy campers. We flew from Houston to New York, Washington, DC, and New Orleans and all over everywhere, in and out of Houston for days, until the airplane had to return to home base for scheduled maintenance. The IPO was not finalized, so the chief passenger searched for another airplane, found one, and asked if I could stay as the flight attendant and see his IPO through to the end. Who was I to say no? I could smell a large paycheck and a large tip! I ended up working on four different airplanes for three weeks and living out of the Marriott Hotel in Houston. I had to go shopping to purchase more clothes and a bathing suit because we took a side excursion to Manzanillo, Mexico, for a little R&R. When we returned to Houston it started all over again. I became very familiar with Houston and New Orleans.

When they finally concluded their business and exhausted me, I was sent packing with a much-hoped-for large tip. I immediately got a ride to the commercial side of the airport and hopped on the first flight heading west. There was a flight to Phoenix about to depart and I took that instead of waiting for a nonstop to Orange County (Santa Ana). I phoned my father and asked him to find me a flight from Phoenix to Santa Ana while I was in the air. That's how anxious I was to get home. When I landed, I was paged in the airport—you know The Voice, not, the-curb-is-for-immediate-loading-and-off-loading voice, but the Patty Hairabedian, (maiden name), please-pick-up-the-white-courtesy-telephone voice. My father was on the line with my next flight information. I was almost home.

MY CHOSEN CAREER AND RELATIONSHIPS

When I arrived, one of my boyfriends was waiting for me with flowers. Boyfriends were never high on my priority list; flying was everything. This career is tough on relationships, for sure. Never knowing whether you're coming or going makes it hard to facilitate a healthy bond. Plus, not spending that much time with one another, even though you've been together for a while, keeps your relationship in its infancy. You think you know someone but you only see the best side of them, because before things have a chance to digress, you are gone. So what you might perceive to be a great relationship is just a temporary arrangement!

One time, the wind gods were favorable to us while

returning to Long Beach from Narita, Japan. Instead of stopping in Anchorage, Alaska, for fuel, as usual, we made it all the way to Seattle, Washington, therefore, cutting off a hefty few hours of flight time. When I got to the house I shared with my boyfriend, I put the key in the door only to see his ex-girlfriend walking down the stairs in my robe!

Trust is something you need in a relationship. If I'm in another country, the boyfriends have free reign to do whatever they want. There's no way you can police them from another continent. Of course, this works both ways!

Another time, I was dating a drummer in a band. When I returned, I would often go to where he was playing. One night he told me not to come. With that, I started making phone calls and found out I had been replaced while I was in New York!

I also think my being a flight attendant contributed to my naiveté in the dating world. Since I really never got to know anyone that closely, I had delusions of grandeur. It was almost like living a fantasy, never knowing what their deep core truths were. I do wonder what would have happened if I had chosen a different career, although I know I'd have never done that.

My career affected my girlfriends too. On a lovely summer day I had a flight to Truckee, Nevada. We were to drop the passengers in Truckee and then fly back to home base and do the same trip to pick the passengers up four days later. My best friend has a vacation home in Lake Tahoe about twenty minutes from the Truckee airport. I was going to get off in Truckee and stay with my friend, then meet the plane in Truckee for the return.

When we got to Truckee, they had closed the airport because a small plane had crashed on landing just before us. We were diverted to Reno. I had no way of contacting my girlfriend until we arrived in Reno.

When she got to Truckee to pick me up, someone told her an airplane had crashed, and it wasn't a good outcome. She demanded to know if it was my plane, but no one could give her any answers. Finally she figured out it wasn't a jet but a light plane, and she guessed I must have gone to Reno. We arrived in Reno and I was worried, trying to call her. Then I heard this familiar voice over the speaker in the FBO. It was her at the gate, asking to be let onto the tarmac.

I couldn't believe she found me: 1. in Reno 2. at the airport in Reno—many FBOs are difficult to find from the street, and 3. in record speed. When I ran to greet her, she jumped out of her car and slapped me across the face! She'd been crying hysterically "I thought you died. How dare you scare me like that!" It was such a genuine moment that I started crying with her. Even the pilots were moved, they were both staring with their jaws on the ground. Did I mention that she is hot too?

Bottom line is this: relationships are definitely a challenge in this business and I learned some tough lessons. I did, however, bring them back some amazing presents!

Chapter 4: What Goes Up Must Come Down

Celebrity Gossip Tidbits

BARBARA WALTERS

Barbara Walters, the first female co-anchor on network news and currently executive producer of the television morning talk show *The View*, was another frequent passenger of mine. Ms. Walters spent the majority of her flights with me frantically writing. Wads of crumpled paper would surround her. When we could, we would keep the papers to unfold later, hoping for juicy gossip or something noteworthy. The only problem was that we couldn't read her handwriting. It's atrocious! Or maybe she knew we were reading it?

DUSTIN HOFFMAN

Dustin Hoffman was traveling in a stateroom with his wife and three children. They were a pleasant, happy, and good-looking family. The youngest of the three children had a sippy cup and it was filled with grape juice. As we got ready for takeoff, the child started to feel queasy and threw up grape juice all over the pink carpet. Dustin Hoffman was extremely apologetic and helped us clean it up. He was very gracious and kind while doing so. At the end of the flight he gave one of the flight attendants a note that read: "Give yourself a raise, because you are the best flight attendants I have ever had." Thank you, kind sir.

BETTE DAVIS

Bette Davis was a revered lifelong movie star. She was nominated for ten Academy Awards and won twice. She was perhaps best known for playing the disturbed Jane in *Whatever Happened to Baby Jane?* Bette Davis was in a stateroom and was traveling with an assistant. They were rehearsing lines for her last film, *The Whales of August*.

It was an uneventful flight that became slightly turbulent. The pilots turned on the "fasten seat belt" sign. One of our flight attendants went into Ms. Davis' stateroom to make sure she had belted herself in. He discovered she hadn't and said to her it was time to fasten up. Ms. Davis interrupted him and said, "Allow me." Then very loudly, "Fasten your seat belts, it's going to be a bumpy night,"—her famous line from the movie *All About Eve*! Never has a flight attendant been more moved, he talked about that for weeks!

JOHNNY CARSON

Johnny Carson did not say "boo" to me, he never said anything at all to me. Even when spoken to, he did not respond. He spent the entire flight in "la-la" land, staring off into space. I would look at him but his wife would answer (I don't know which wife this was). His wife answered every single question on a five hour flight. Johnny never even looked at me. It was very, very odd and I have no explanation for it whatsoever.

JAMES GARNER and JASON PRIESTLY

When I was flying on a Gulfstream for a private corporation, we would often hit the Indy circuit—Indianapolis

Racing League. We would usually leave Southern California on Thursday morning and return home the Sunday after the race. On the Sunday flights, I would typically order extra catering because my boss had a tendency to bring more people with him to the airplane that had not been on the outbound flight. James Garner and Jason Priestley, both car-racing enthusiasts would often hitch a ride home with us.

James Garner—"Jim Rockford" of *The Rockford Files* and star of *The Notebook*—was always early. He was usually the first one to the airplane. He would always pick an inconspicuous seat away from the core of the "party." He was quiet, polite, sort of tranquil, and gracious as can be. He never cared what he ate and when asked, always answered, "Whatever you have the most of." I always thought he must be an excellent husband and father. It seemed like nothing was about him, even though he could have easily made everything about him.

Speaking of Indy, do you know how many private jets are on the ground during the Indianapolis 500? When you are departing on the Sunday after the race (with everyone else) it is a chaotic mess. The airplanes are lined up wing to wing like a sea of "bugs". Finding yours is always challenging! Once, I walked around the tarmac for over thirty minutes looking for my airplane. I finally went back to the FBO, found a ramper (they tow, fuel, help with luggage, etc.) and hitched a ride on a golf cart until we found it. Actually, this happens frequently with sport events of this magnitude. Whether the Super Bowl, the Masters, the Olympics, the World Series or any other major event, the FBO's at the nearest airport will be saturated with private jets. It's usually the only time I get to see other flight attendants that the pilots have told me about, but I had never met – we are always in the air! But it's also difficult to get your dishes back, get your catering, get your perishables out of the refrigerator, get fuel and get the heck out of there. Like I said - chaotic mess.

Since, I'm digressing, let's go the opposite way. One time we dropped our passengers at a different airport then flew to our home base and taxied to the hangar. But no one was there and the hangar was locked. They forgot about us! We were locked in the airport. We could not get into the hangar or our cars. We were staring at our cars on the opposite side of a very large and formidable fence. We could not climb over, we could not go around, we were stuck *inside* the airport. I was going to see "Chicago" play live that night with my dear friends and I was not going be late. I am never late.

We didn't know what to do, so we started making cocktails. If we had an APU: auxiliary power unit, we would have hooked up ground power and turned on music and lights as well, but that was locked in the hangar. This is also known as an "APU party". Which we do sometimes while cleaning the aircraft after landing.

We called all the FBOs on the field but they were of no use to us, except for laughing at our predicament. Finally we got a hold of airport security who arrived to let us out but not without a snicker and a chuckle. And the jet had to sit outside all night, poor baby.

One time we were taxing in and there was all this activity in the hangar. Somebody came rushing out and told us to kill the engines, we were ruining their shot. *"What?" "What the hell you talking about?"* The pilots killed the engines and we peered out the front windshield to see what was going on. There was a film crew in there and they were shooting a scene from a television show. Well, that was great, but I had dishes to do and an airplane to clean – so get the heck out of my way.

I opened the door and began to do my usual clean up. I carried my dishes in a dirty dish bin to the kitchen where I intended to wash them. Then out of the corner of my left eye, I see this guy running up to me and he is not happy. He yelled that my high heels on the hangar floor were clicking and ruined their shot *again*! *"Well, excuse me!"* I had walked as close to the right wall as possible – I had to do my dishes! And after all, this was my planes hangar. He didn't quite see it that way. Anyway, the airplane ended up being in a scene from a very popular television show. Yikes, I have truly digressed.

CHERYL TIEGS AND MARY TYLER MOORE

Like I said, on Regent Air the action was in the staterooms. After meal service, we would make up the beds and shut the curtains and the passengers could sleep the remainder of the flight. In this era, nothing out of the ordinary was surprising. Many passengers just plain told us to stay out of the stateroom, period. But if we were starting descent, then we were required to disturb the occupants to begin preparations for landing. Especially, if we had made up the beds, it took a while to restore them into their original club seats

When I went to awaken the most recognizable *Sports Illustrated* swimsuit edition model, Cheryl Tiegs, a little dog came bounding from under the bed ready to attack. I was shocked, I had no idea there was a dog in there. The little runt of a dog must have been in her carry-on, and I was not privy to this. She had secured the tiny thing to the airplane and he was snoozing under the bed. When I walked into the stateroom, he was startled and went into miniature attack mode. Cheryl Tiegs jumped out of the bed with a tiny nighty all askew to shush him. I stood there like an idiot and stared. She grabbed the dog and dived under the covers. I think we were both embarrassed!

There were many little dogs on my flights, before it became fashionable to have a doggy with you everywhere you went. Mary Tyler Moore, the famous actress from the show bearing her name, was another frequent flier who always had her tiny dogs with her. But with Mary Tyler Moore and most others, we knew about them!

LUCILLE BALL

All through my career flying around the world, I was fortunate to be with wonderful people. It's awfully difficult to spend so much time with someone you don't respect or admire, regardless of whether they're passengers or crew. I had been lucky enough not to have to fly with very many mean-spirited people. I heard horror stories from other flight crew all the time. I tried to be impervious to these tales until I could come to my own conclusions. Usually, though, they turned out to be true. It was always a huge letdown when the people you couldn't wait to meet were, in fact, jerks.

I was so excited to fly with Lucille Ball myself, but I had heard horrible stories about her from everybody. Before I got my opportunity to see if the rumors were true, she was banned from Regent Air. Apparently, she was a total bitch, I guess that's why they call it *acting.*

CAROLE CHANNING AND ELVIRA

Singer, actress, and comedian Carole Channing is probably best known for her *Hello Dolly* role. She boarded a flight with two hatboxes in her arms and a turban around her head. She tried to strap the hatboxes into seats around her, but I told her they must be stored in the closet for takeoff. She looked at me and said, "Be careful, Honey. Carole Channing is in there." When I was out of sight, I looked inside the boxes and sure enough Carole Channing's hair, or more appropriately wigs, were inside.

Elvira, "Mistress of the Dark," boarded another flight with many hatboxes. I had no idea who she was. Standing in front of me was an adorable redhead. I did not recognize her name or face without all the makeup and that hair. When I was out of her line of vision, I peeked inside the hatboxes, and yes, Elvira was in there too.

ROBERT DE NIRO

Robert De Niro, the academy award-winning "Godfather," was seated in the front cabin on Regent Air. Remember I said some of the seats weren't as desirable as others. He was opposite a stranger in front of him and an elderly couple across the aisle. He felt they were all staring at him. He actually said to them, "Stop staring at me!" He begged us to move him, which after several tense minutes of seat juggling, we were able to do. I guess people staring at you all the time would get old.

STEVE MARTIN

Speaking of staring, comedian and famous actor Steve

Martin was on one of my flights. He has the BEST skin I have

ever seen on a man. It is almost translucent. It was difficult not to

stare at him. I should have asked him what his secret is!

VAN HALEN

On one flight I was so excited to have rock stars! Van

Halen, known for some pretty original rock and roll and

tumultuous antics, were *the* band at the time. Eddy Van Halen

and David Lee Roth were best pals then and were partying and

laughing while we soared across the country. When I pushed

open their curtain, Eddy handed me a straw. I had no idea what

that was for until I looked down and saw the lines of cocaine on

the tray table. Although, I had never seen the stuff before, it

wasn't hard to figure out. I politely excused myself saying I

didn't indulge. In the 80's, there were no drug tests for flight

crew and everyone in every walk of life was partying up a storm.

It wouldn't be unheard of if a flight attendant did do drugs with

the passengers. I had heard stories that this (amongst other

things) had been happening on other flights. They were cool with me not joining them, but wanted to make sure I would bring them beer. And so I did. They ran me for beer every twenty minutes. Every time I came within earshot of them, they yelled for beer. I was constantly putting warm beer in the ice to stay ahead of them. At last, we just ran out. They drank every last beer on that airplane, which was no easy task!

Incidentally, Van Halen had a rider in their contract for the venues where they would play concerts. Apparently, one of the requests was that a bowl of M&Ms be put in their dressing room with all the brown M&Ms removed! They asked for that because they wanted to be sure the rest of the contract had been honored, as there were legitimate safety concerns. The M&Ms were only an insurance policy, so to speak, that the contract had been read in full. Maybe the producers on Tom Cruise's flight caught wind of this and decided to jump on the bandwagon? Weird coincidence—or was it?

MERV GRIFFIN

I was called at the last minute to do a 5:00 am "show

time" for a jet that was an hour and a half away from me. I awakened at 2:30 am, got ready and drove and made my 5:00 am show time. I can *never* be late, so I arrived about 4:45am, maybe even 4:30-ish.

That was great, but no one was at the FBO. I walked around, all the doors were locked, the hangar was locked. Everything was locked. It was freezing, but I had my favorite giant big green "squishy" coat that I bought in Quebec, Canada (one of the coldest places I've been). So I sat in front of the doors until somebody finally opened them. But I still couldn't get into the aircraft, which was locked to. So I waited and waited and waited. At least I had coffee.

I finally got into the airplane, when I walked in, I was dumbstruck. This beautiful private jet was a disaster! First of all- it stank a horrid stench. It was a mess. There were dirty dishes and crap all over the galley. The cabin was equally as messy. Blankets and pillows all thrown about, crumpled newspapers and papers strewn everywhere.

170

I began to clean it up – I mean who else was going to? I opened the dirty ice drawer and almost gagged. I had to hold my nose, while I collected all the room temperature milk and every other stinky thing in there. Then I scrubbed it with vinegar which took me forever to find in the hangar (all private jets use vinegar some place). It was nasty.

I thought to myself, *"they only called me to clean this mess up!"* After I cleaned it up as best I could with my limited time frame, I looked around and noticed, nobody took care of this plane – I'm sure it didn't have a regular flight attendant. It needed an interior face lift so bad, it was sad. The couch desperately needed to be replaced. The galley needed to be re-done completely. The lavatory was disgusting as well. Who lets a 30 million private jet go to hell?

Anyway, I almost didn't fly it, because I was thinking about the mechanical situation. After talking to the pilots, I was assured the plane was flying worthy and I went with them. I was disappointed that it was friends of Merv's and not him, but what

171

are you going to do? That's how this business is.

I flew some really nice people to Mexico and dropped them off. On the way back, I scrubbed that plane until my fingers were raw. And I told the pilots that someone had to give a crap about the interior even if Merv Griffin didn't!

MICHAEL LANDON

Bonanza and *Little House on the Prairie* alumni, Michael Landon, and his family were on a Regent Air flight in the morning. He was adorable as expected, but he was not very talkative. He was rather cold and standoffish, and I was very cautious around them. I felt as if I was bothering them even though I was bringing them food and drink. Michael Landon did not eat, he explained to me he didn't eat breakfast or lunch. He didn't eat all day on the set, so when he returned home he could have a large meal with his family. I guess this was to keep his weight in check and maybe to keep his family in check. He was very svelte and thin. The family part of the plan I'm not too sure about because after the meal service I served his son, who was just a toddler, a bowl of ice cream and he threw it at me! Seriously, chocolate ice cream all over my uniform! I was waiting for some kind of a reaction from him or his wife, but they brushed it off, like it was no big deal that their son throws ice cream at people. Please.

LANA TURNER

Lana Turner was a huge film star mainly from the 1940s and 1950s, although she worked much of her life. Early in her career she was often cast opposite Clark Gable. Her most famous role was most likely *The Postman Always Rings Twice*. She was another famous movie star who was married eight times, although most people think this unique to Elizabeth Taylor.

Lana was on a morning flight on Regent Air. She asked for caviar, which was fine, we served it, just not in the morning. That did not sit well with her. She had been told we served caviar and she gosh-darn wanted some! She threw a fit—she wanted caviar. There was a small amount of mayhem while the chief purser tried to acquire caviar. Well, this is the rich and famous and if they want caviar at eight o'clock in the morning, then they should have it! Somehow the chief purser managed to get the caterers to the aircraft in record time with her caviar. The flight left twenty minutes late, but I am sure had we not gotten the caviar, she would have been difficult the entire flight.

GUESS JEANS: MARCIANO BROTHERS

The Marciano brothers were in the beginning of their amazing career. Their "Guess" jean line was just beginning its rise to fame and was yet to flourish into the brand it is today. There were four Marciano brothers, Georges, Paul, Maurice, and Armand, who traveled together. The eldest—the decision maker—led them.

When I asked for a beverage order, the eldest answered first, regardless of who I was looking at. He replied, "Coffee black," and then the next brother answered, "Yes, coffee black," and then the next brother, "Yes, coffee black," and the last brother, "Yes, coffee black." It was all said so fast as if it was a comedy sketch, but of course it wasn't. When it was time to take their lunch order, the exact same thing happened. I couldn't help giggling to myself, because I knew they didn't do it on purpose, it was just how they were. They weren't laughing, but I was dying inside, trying to suppress a full core meltdown because it was hilarious! Every course, the exact same thing happened.

If I did not have four of something, I never offered it to the Marciano Brothers as I knew whatever the eldest brother wanted, the others would follow suit. I guess it was respect for your eldest brother that traveled down the lineage?

OJ SIMPSON and MENENDEZ BROTHERS

Well before all three of them ended up in prison, they flew with us on Regent Air. Before OJ was considered a murderer by most, he was actually a pretty nice guy. He always had a smile on his face and was very polite – How's that for an oxy-moron!

The Menendez brothers flew with us many times – with their parents. And yes they were alive. Why would you kill your parents when there are taking you on private jets? Hell, I'm glad

I made it out alive.

ROBERT EARL

I was flying on a Gulfstream out of Burbank for Planet Hollywood. Robert Earl started the Planet Hollywood restaurants after leaving the presidency of the Hard Rock Cafés amid a huge scandal. It seemed that the Hard Rock Café was pissed-off that Planet Hollywood had "stolen" its theme. Robert Earl was my sole passenger. He was angry because his pasta was not al dente. Okay, mister, we are at 36,000 feet in two percent humidity, did you want to consider that? He was condescending, rude, and full of himself. He was the only passenger I refused to fly again.

ESTER WILLIAMS AND EDIE ADAMS

I had these two women on a flight, and they were absolutely delightful. I had no idea who they were. The next night I was watching a movie with my mother and I recognized Ester Williams. Ester Williams is a retired competitive swimmer and movie star from the 1940s and 1950s. She is known for "aqua musicals." Edie Adams was the sexpot actress, singer, and comedian from the same era as Ester Williams. Ester Williams was Lorenzo Lamas' stepmother, who also did a stint on *Celebrity Apprentice*.

I had driven out to my parents' to spend the weekend with them at our lake house. It was really cute because as I was watching the movie, I piped up, "Hey, I flew that woman last night! She was with Edie Adams, and they were so much fun.

GUESS WHO

I was called for a four-day charter to take this man and his posse to perform two shows. This man is the most clever, smartest, fastest thinking brilliant comedian I have ever been lucky enough to see (and fly). The lot of them were so dang funny, I had a permanent smile on my face and have never laughed so loud, spontaneously and often on any charter, ever. It would be impossible to fly with these men and not break out into hysterical laughter; I would bet my life savings that no one could remain straight faced. He drank Bailey's Irish Crème on the rocks stating, "Real men drink Bailey's!"

These guys had me rolling, continuously. Then they gave myself and the two pilots tickets to the second show, I would have not missed it for all the green tea in China. This man and his entourage are the most unbelievable comic genius ever. I am convinced this was the wittiest man I have ever flown. And way underrated for his mental brilliance.

MORNING NEWSCASTER LOS ANGELES

This gal came on board just as real as could be, just like you would expect after watching her on television. She's exceptionally gorgeous with an awesome and quick personality and I liked her immediately. She was wearing four-inch platform high heels that, although adorable, looked painful. We had a short forty-five-minute flight and I only served her a cup of coffee. When we arrived I told her to be careful exiting the airplane because the stairs would be slippery and she was wearing those giant shoes.

When she got to the bottom stair: she fell, landed on her side, looked up at me, winked, laughed, then jumped in the waiting limousine, and shut the door.

While watching her show the Monday after the weekend I flew with her, she was talking about how great flying on a private jet is and then referred to me as a "ditz." Thanks for that!

GUESS WHO

We had one incredibly wealthy and famous celebrity on Regent Air who loved champagne. After draining a few glasses, she became impatient for a refill and moseyed up to the bar to procure some more of the exquisite bubbly. The food and beverage flight attendant began to open a new bottle of champagne for this well-known woman. As he started to tear at the foil, our illustrious lady began to stroke the neck of the bottle in an erotic fashion, over and over again. No words were spoken between them, just he unwrapping and her stroking.

Then the cork "popped," she looked at him and said,

"I'm done" and released her grip on the bottle to await the tasting of the nectar.

CELIBRITY RE-HAB

Yes, I have flown a couple celebrities to rehabilitation centers. I would never put their names in print as I believe we all need a little help now and then, they should be applauded –not exploited.

THE GOLFERS

Many of my rich and famous clients enjoy the game of golf. I have flown with golf professionals around the circuit of tournaments. I have flown with golf fanatics to the legendary courses where they couldn't wait to get off the plane. I have done Midwest golf tours where the courses were literally located in the middle of nowhere and we were lucky to find a crappy motel. I had such serious golf enthusiasts that they wore their golf shoes on the plane.

I've been to St. Andrews in Scotland, and to its closest

replica in Coos Bay, Oregon, more than once, more than I can count. I've been to the Masters several times. The Masters is the

first of four major golf championships played every year on the same course. The Masters is most famously known (other than the difficulty of the course) for the players' green jackets, which were originally intended to differentiate the players from the patrons. It's also known for being held on the second Sunday in April, which sometimes lands on Easter Sunday. It is located in Augusta, Georgia, and it is a beautiful area, very green and lush. There are tons of weeping willows and other "bent" trees with every shade of green on the planet, everywhere you look.

One of my layovers in Augusta, I stayed in the most authentic Bed and Breakfast Inn. This B&B was one of my favorites of all the bizarre places I have slept around the world. It had a four-post bed four feet off the floor, complete with mosquito net and squeaky mattress. There was an inviting fireplace hearth with a settee for afternoon tea, and the tiniest, yet cutest bathroom. Beyond the charming French doors, was an alluring balcony where you could watch the activity on the street below or just enjoy the greenery surrounding you. It was as if you were plucked out of this century and placed back in time a hundred years ago in an old classic story. I adored that room and didn't want to leave.

One time, I was called for a last minute charter to the Masters. Dispatch had booked us a room, but it was in this gross motel. As soon as we got to the parking lot, we all looked at each other and said, "Hmm, I'm thinking there is no way we are staying here." We did get out of the car and looked in one of the rooms hoping maybe it would be tolerable, it wasn't. We decided to find our own rooms. Just to give you an idea of how much of a draw the Masters is: we drove for hours and could not find a room. We finally ended up in South Carolina in one of our most beloved Marriott's. Thank you, Marriott, you have saved my life many times around the world.

While on the subject of hotels, I'll tell you that most of them were fabulous but some of them have been awful. On an overnight in Dublin, Ireland for crew rest, my room was about as big as a trailer bathroom. The shower was actually over the toilet! Plus I've been to motels where I slept in my jeans and T-shirt rather than touch those sheets. I even showered in my flip-flops. I've also managed to live through at least six or eight hotel fire alarms and scrambled down stairs in the middle of the night with my favorite old, well-used Lakers T-shirt that was probably not the most appropriate attire. Not to mention, locking myself out of countless hotel rooms in that T-shirt.

One time I was in my room and went out on the balcony to enjoy the view. I shut the slider to keep the air-conditioned room cool. When I decided to go back into the room, I couldn't open the slider. Okay. Wait a minute—I must have not pulled hard enough. I tried again and again. That door wasn't budging. Are you kidding me? I am locked out of my own room on my own balcony? What the hell? What am I gonna do?

I was on the second floor, so I figured I could shimmy down over the side. I scrambled over the side, hanging by my hands with the intention of jumping to the bushes below. Are you getting a visual on this? Uh, no can do. I would have broken an ankle, it was just too far and I had to fly the next day—flying being more important than broken ankle (stupid, eh?). Plus the rough concrete of the patio was digging into my fingers and palms. So I climbed back up and reassessed my situation.

It was noisy because I was close to a freeway, but I figured I could start screaming and someone was bound to hear me. I started screaming and yelling but no one heard me. Okay, I'll have to jump. My hands hurt from hanging last time, but I didn't have a choice, so over the side I went. The same thing happened. I knew if I let go, something had to break my fall and that something was going to be part of my body. I climbed back up and this time my hands really hurt. I did what girls do best: I started crying. That helped a lot.

Okay, reassess, I have to yell and scream louder. No one heard me, there was no one around. Now I am starting to pace and cry and freak out, I'd been locked out for over an hour, and it was getting dark. Then out of my peripheral vision, I noticed some smoke coming from far off to the right. Aha! Someone is smoking on their balcony! I have never yelled louder in my life. I reached octaves of screaming I didn't know I had in me. Then a guy leaned over the side of his balcony. I tried to yell to him that I was locked out, but he couldn't hear me. I finally just shrieked, "Help" I guess that got through to him because ten minutes later some hotel employee showed up beneath my balcony and I frantically explained my situation. He broke out into laughter—which totally pissed me off. This was not funny. Another ten minutes went by and then to my great relief there was a maintenance man on the other side of my slider. In whole, I was outside for almost two hours. Does this kind of stuff happen to anybody else? Why do I feel like the Lone Ranger on this?

But back to the golfers. I had one famous professional golfer who was a blast to fly with. He always had a "squeezy" ball in his hand—you know the ones the golfers use to strengthen their forearms? I flew him several times and I never saw him with out his squeezy ball. On the way home from Hawaii once, he told me "As soon as we get back, I am going to Europe." *Ok that's' nice,* I thought and then he continued, "I have to get lamb placenta injected into my neck!" Apparently, lamb placenta is the fountain of youth and/or improves your golf game. Now you all know the secret!

I wish I would have paid more attention to the golfers than I did. I never really knew who they were, other than golfers, pathetic—I know.

HOLIDAYS

I love holidays. It's a delightful diversion from the everyday flying the rich and famous on a private jet. Well – just like you and your career, after a while it becomes monotonous.

For instance: Halloween, I love Halloween! I used to play scary music, put dry ice in their drinks - I even wore a giant witch hat. And one *must* decorate for Halloween. I put spider webs all over with little spiders clinging to them. The passengers loved it, but not more than I. 186

Easter one year, I had a family with little children. I decided to make a scavenger hunt for the kids with a chocolate bunny at the end. It was a long flight and when you have little children, they get bored! I can't tell you how many times I've played "Go Fish". The scavenger hunt was a blast, however, chocolate bunnies on a forty million dollar private jet - not my best idea.

Christmas is the easiest. I would put a tiny live Christmas tree on the credenza instead of flowers, with little presents underneath. It would make the cabin smell delightful. I put Christmas carols on for boarding music and on the bulkhead, I had put up little stockings with the passengers names written on them. I bribed the pilots to wear Santa hats with my fresh baked cookies, And an apple pie in the oven never hurt.

Hawaii was always fun too. I always made Mai-Tai's with Hawaiian boarding music playing. On the return, I would have lei's for the women and coconut shell beads for the men. I have been to Hawaii countless times - go ahead you're allowed to be envious! Even Veterans Day, I would put little American flag tooth picks in the passenger's sandwiches if I knew they were veterans.

One thing you must keep in mind: you have to know your passengers ethnicity. If you get that wrong, you're going to have a miserable trip. If you don't know, you don't do anything!

Every day of your life, you can choose to make it fun or not. I always chose to make it fun when I was flying. I mean, I was on a private jet, what did I have to complain about?

Chapter 5: Another Day in Paradise

Exciting Layovers

There's great diversity among pilots and attendants. Some are young and full of energy; some are old and not overly enthusiastic. In the aviation industry there are folks we call slam clickers. Slam clickers are pilots and/or flight attendants who "slam the door and click the lock", meaning they don't want to do anything with you on a layover. In the case of a slam-clicker, you may never see them at all during a layover until "checked out and ready to go" for the next flight. Or the opposite may happen, if they aren't slam clickers, then you may not be able to shake them the entire time. You could also have any mixture in between someone who wants to go and do anything and someone who wants to stay in the hotel the entire layover.

Our flights were usually long, so you'd have time for a conversation or two, or eighteen. Generally, by the end of the that leg, you knew what everyone may or may not want to do while on layover. If you've been flying with the same pilots a lot, you also know that their wife serves meatloaf on Thursdays or that the bougainvillea won't grow on the south side of their house. You know if they eat breakfast or not, if they work out or not, if they are drinkers or not, if they are early birds or night owls. You get the picture.

One thing they all have in common is they get tired of sitting in those seats for hours and hours. Many of them have bad backs too, so I learned to perfect the "elbow" back rub. I can usually rub out those sore spots until they scream. The other thing we all have in common is the love of aviation.

When traveling with a familiar crew, we usually came up with something to go looking for in each layover. One crew I flew with always went searching for the best chicken wings. Another crew was looking for the perfect key lime pie. It's fun to rate them and continue the search for a better one. It gave us something to look forward to, especially if we were going to a city we'd been to several times, we'd expand our search.

During layovers, we have gone to famous places like the Great Pyramids and Mt. Rushmore - these types of places are always first on the list of things to do while on layover. We also visited museums. I have been to some amazing museums. I have toured the Smithsonian at least a dozen times and still haven't seen all of it—I can never get the pilots out of the aviation exhibit! Go figure.

Zoos: this one's usually a crew pleaser, especially the one we went to in Sydney, Australia for obvious reasons. Tours: especially wineries and breweries, another crew pleaser. Movies are usually at the bottom of the list, normally when we're bored. Shopping: most of the pilots don't want to go unless it's their wife's birthday and they need help, although many have gone with me to bazaar-type places.

Plays or the theatre are fun, especially if the chief passenger has given us tickets, which were usually excellent seats. Bowling: only if we were utterly bored out of our minds.

Air shows: jackpot! Horse, car, and dog races: depends on how convenient and whether or not we're "connected." Jet skiing, water skiing, surfing, wind surfing: any of these are winners. Rollerblading, hiking, mountain biking, touring on foot: again, all winners. Golf tournaments: great but tricky because we're usually leaving the day of the event. Snow skiing: my personal favorite, but hard to get anybody to go with me. Fine dining: one has to eat.

And finally, red light districts: There are some hosts who can't wait to show you around—all around. We were in Saipan once, and they took us to the most outrageous show. The girls were really young, and I learned they were working to send money back to their families. It was appalling to say the least, but it was *quite* a show. A much better choice on Saipan: the best waterslide ever!

Key West, Florida

On a gorgeous warm, sunny, and humid day we were on a layover in the Florida Keys and decided to rent Sea-Doos. We were having a marvelous time riding alone and with each other and goofing around. At one point I had my chief pilot behind me on my Sea-Doo, as I cut a sharp turn to maneuver a 360, he went flying off the back. To my astonishment, when he came up I was headed straight for him and hit him in the head—really hard. He had quite the headache after that. I was fearful I would never fly with that flight department again, but thankfully, he forgave me.

Cleveland, Ohio

Another time, I begged my all-time favorite pilot and dear, dear friend, to drive with me from Toledo, Ohio, an hour and a half to Cleveland to visit the Rock and Roll Hall of Fame. I had been dying to do this my entire career but had never been near Cleveland. I figured Toledo was close enough. We only had four hours to spend there because we had to turn around and come back the same day. To really enjoy the Rock and Roll Hall of Fame, one really needs a whole day at the very least, I could have spent a week! It was so worth it, at least for me, I enjoyed every minute of the four hours we were there and the three hours we were in the car!

New York City, New York

The pilots at Regent Air were kind enough to let me stop on the way to the airplane and pick up prepared but uncooked New York pizzas. Really, is there any other kind of pizza? I would put the pizzas in the aft air stairs where they would freeze. When I returned to Southern California, I would invite my friends over and cook them. My friends began to know my flight schedule in anticipation of the much-loved pizza. Most of them had never had *real* New York pizza.

Nagoya, Japan

When I first arrived in Nagoya, Japan, the company I was flying for had prearranged a bilingual woman to show us the lay of the land. She was also going to accompany me shopping for the airplane. But, we still had a cultural barrier—it's difficult when there are so many cultural differences.

You don't want to offend anyone, yet a common habit

194

may indeed offend. You're kind of afraid to get comfortable or relax because you might blow it like burp loudly or use a hand gesture that's considered rude in another culture. Because of this we really wanted to be on our own when we got to the hotel. We were off duty, at least until the next flight. But sometimes we don't have a choice.

We were invited to a special dinner, which again we didn't really want to go to, but we were the guests of honor. We sat down at this elaborate table and tried to make conversation as best we could with the very limited Japanese we knew and their limited English. One of the pilots was speaking so loudly, I kept kicking him under the table. You know how when you're speaking to someone and they don't understand, you speak louder? Like that will help them understand? He was embarrassing.

As we were making our way through several courses of all kinds of foods, we were served a bird. The bird was hollowed out and stuffed with—well, I don't know what it was stuffed with, probably bird. It still had its feathers and was basically intact except for the eyes and innards. We knew enough etiquette to know we had to at least try the bird, but we also knew there was no way in hell we were eating bird. They wouldn't bring the next course if you hadn't finished the current one, and it seemed like we would never get through this dinner.

Smart chick that I am, I told one of my pilots to ask where the bathroom was and pretend he didn't understand which really took no pretending at all. This would require the translator's attention and create a diversion. While this was happening, I quickly scooped part of his bird and mine into my napkin and crammed it in my purse. The other pilot ate his bird and announced his delight with it—talk about a brown-noser!

Guatemala City, Guatemala

We were booked into a Marriott Hotel one time in Guatemala City. We only had a couple days and were told to stay in the hotel no matter what—which is always impossible for me to do. Yet going outside the hotel was not encouraged.

196

When I arrived at my room, I opened the curtains to see the view and there was a Chuck E. Cheese's across the street. I was not expecting this, not in the least. It was odd. I went downstairs to meet the pilots and noticed many children in strollers. Then I noticed there were some "different" kinds of adults with these children.

The pilots and I were eating in the hotel restaurant and it became more obvious that the hotel catered to children in many ways. And every age group of children, from infants to older kids. I am probably one of the most curious people on the planet and decided to find out what the deal was.

I talked the pilots into having an after dinner drink in the lobby where I could hopefully find some adults willing to answer my questions. I found the sweetest couple with a toddler and an infant and I just asked them, "What's the deal?"

Apparently, if the United States or other countries have rejected you as adoptive parents, Guatemala is where you go. They explained to me some strange rules like you have to stay in

Guatemala with the children for two weeks and then go home, childless. You can come back in one month and take the child home after some money is exchanged. If you want the child to have a United States passport then you have to come back and stay longer or pay more money or something to that effect. Anyhow, it explained the Chuck E. Cheese.

As I have told you, I'm not one to stay in the hotel. So my favorite pilot and I went walking around outside the hotel, although we didn't go far because it was kind of creepy, if only because there were so many children begging for money. They lined the sidewalks and pushed and shoved and begged. I really couldn't take it—it was so desperately sad.

Tokyo, Japan

Another adventure in dining in Japan was in a restaurant resembling a sushi bar. Instead of sushi we were served bamboo skewers with panko-fried food. There were one or two bite-size pieces of food per bamboo stick. Some things I recognized by taste or consistency like mushrooms or vegetables. But some were slimy and disgusting. Most of them were unidentifiable.

The Japanese believe one should eat at least thirty different kinds of food per day, although fifty is desirable. Now I don't think they were trying to feed us fifty kinds of food, but I think if one wanted to eat fifty kinds of food, the panko parade is the place to be. We had not a clue of what we were eating, nor how to stop the endless surprise on a stick without being rude. I just swallowed it down with a swig of beer.

Finally after consuming many glasses of beer to wash down the mystery food, our chief pilot put an end to it by expressing his desire to see a karaoke bar. So off to karaoke we went. I think it's a requirement that you're not able to carry a tune if you karaoke in Japan. Everybody is terrible, and it's so hilarious! It is so humbling and accepting; everyone is just singing and laughing and de-stressing, I suppose. We were no different. We were belting out tunes with the worst of them, and it was a delightfully good time.

The next morning, I was packing to deadhead back to the

United States and I broke a nail. When I opened my Crazy Glue, the glue came flying out straight into my eye. The pressure from the airplane had obviously built up and it was strong. My eye began to water like crazy and my makeup began to run down my face. When the pilots saw me, they were extremely worried. I looked like someone punched me, and black mascara was everywhere. They were concerned and thought I should see an ophthalmologist, but I insisted on getting back to the United States. We were heading to Anchorage overnight, so I suggested I could wait until we got there. We landed in Anchorage around two in the morning and the chief pilot took me to the emergency room while the other pilot "put the airplane to bed." The doctor determined there was no permanent damage, but I had to wear a patch for a week and was teased mercilessly by the pilots.

New Orleans, Louisiana

On a layover in New Orleans it began to rain, and rain, and rain harder. It eventually escalated to a full-blown drenching downpour. We had already decided we were going to have dinner at the famous landmark restaurant Commander's Palace. Eager to experience the restaurant and not wishing to stay in the hotel, we decided to go despite all the rain. But, we did opt for a taxi instead of our planned trolley ride.

We had been shown to a table on the second floor and were delighted with the ambience, although it was really raining sideways against the building by now. We ordered and were chatting while we waited for our food. And all of the sudden, the lights went out. We had candlelight from the tables, but the staff quickly lit more. And then the server brought our entrées. He said that our plates were the last to come out of the kitchen before the power went out.

It was a delicious dinner but a wild night. A few minutes later the manager announced to all the patrons that basically the whole city was flooded and we would have to spend the night in the restaurant. Uh—I don't think so. There was no way we were going to spend the night in this restaurant. We went downstairs and were greeted by four feet of water inside the restaurant. Oh man, this was bad.

We went outside and discovered that the water was flowing very swiftly over the tops of the parking meters. You could just make out the top two or three inches of the parking meters. There were no cars moving and obviously no trolleys, just water rushing by. It was radical—I'd never seen anything like this, ever. Then I noticed what looked like a hotel shuttle bus that was kind of moving, but only a foot or so at a time. The bus was going forward and then it would stop. Then it would back up. We couldn't figure out what the bus was doing. Since it was the only moving thing on the road, we decided to investigate.

I had a three-quarter-length summer dress. In order to cross the street and the hastening water, I had to tie my dress up at my waist. There I was, exposing my panties to everyone, but I was not sleeping in the restaurant. I was determined to get back to the hotel, as were the pilots. It was hard to stay upright because the water current was so strong. I only had the top third of my body out of the water, not to mention fighting torrents of rain in my face. But I made it.

When we got to the door of the bus, we banged on it, it opened, and I jumped in. Inside were six drunk Texan oil tycoons! They exclaimed, "All right, the dancer is here!" The pilots stood there with this stupid look on their face, not believing these good ol' boys were ogling me while they were standing there taking Mother Nature's abuse.

We finally learned from the driver that the bus had a wheel stuck in the trolley tracks. It was immovable, couldn't go forward, and couldn't go back. I quickly negotiated a deal that if we would help them off the tracks, they would give us a ride back to Bourbon Street where our hotel was. It was a great tradeoff, although the Texans were disappointed that I would not leave my dress tied up.

One of the pilots stayed out in the drenching rain to guide the bus while the other pilot shouted commands to the driver. Then just like that, the bus was free. Now we had to make our way from the Garden District to the French Quarter. It's only a short cab ride, but it took two hours that night. The driver was afraid of getting trapped on the trolley tracks again, plus he couldn't see anything in front of him. The rain was fierce and blinding. We eventually got back to the hotel where we discovered water in the lobby but that was as far as it went. Fortunately, our rooms were dry.

After we arrived home in Southern California, we learned that eighteen inches of rain had fallen in six hours. Five people died and 250 guests had to be rescued from, well, hmmm, go ahead make a guess. You got it: Commander's Palace.

Abaco, Bahamas

We had started this trip out of Long Beach, California, and were to reposition the jet to Portland, Oregon, to pick up passengers on a commercial airline. Then we were to fly to Treasure Cay, which is Abaco, Bahamas. The Abaco islands are located on the northern side of the Bahamas and are known for sailing and boating. I can tell you that their beaches are pretty amazing as well, pearly white sand and beautiful crystal clear water. Apparently the coral reefs aren't too shabby either.

We were due to arrive after sunset. Treasure Cay is not usually open in the evening due to the heavy drug trafficking that is so prevalent throughout the Bahamas. But, of course, they made special arrangements for a private jet of our status. There was no fuel at Treasure Cay, so the pilots had to ascertain the amount we would require to insure our return to Ft. Lauderdale, Florida, in order to clear customs and purchase additional fuel.

I had buttoned up the cabin and was sitting in my jump seat between the two pilots when we began our descent into Abaco. As often happens in this business, we ended up arriving well after sunset. I began to listen to the pilots intently because they believed we were indeed above the airport but did not have it "in sight." It was pitch black beneath us. Nor was anyone answering the radio. We began to circle what we believed to be the airport beneath us, while constantly asking for advisement from the ground. Finally, we received a radio call asking if we were the aircraft they were expecting. Why, yes we were, would you mind turning on some lights? The airport has lights; they just don't use them to discourage drug smugglers.

Now we began our approach onto the runway. Everything seemed normal until about half the lights went out. Fortunately, we were still able to complete the approach and landed safely. It was only after parking the aircraft that the pilots had discovered what the issue with the lights was. Since the airport was rarely used, the local foliage had begun to grow abundant and had grown over the lights! Needless to say, we were all relieved to be on the ground. And I'm sure Treasure Cay realized they had some serious gardening to attend to.

After putting the airplane "to bed," our greeting committee of one drove us to our hotel, which turned out to be individual condominiums right on the beach. We hurried to change and get to the bar for our much-anticipated drink. When we found the bar there was only the bartender, one other patron and our "greeter." The greeter or host was explaining to us that the drink in the Bahamas was a "Green Bay Smasher" and that we really needed to try it. Well—when in Rome. So we each had a Green Bay Smasher. And then we had another one. Maybe more than another one, I don't really remember. But it became quite apparent why they are entitled "Smashers."

The bartender was in no mood and wanted to close up, so we went to explore this unknown little paradise. We had barely even looked at our accommodations. We went down to the water and stuck our toes in and marveled at how warm it was and how beautiful the entire setting was. It was tranquil, so very tranquil. It seemed like a place that was lost in time, raw and unspoiled. We couldn't wait to get out on the beach the next day.

After finishing what was left of our Smashers, we all three went to look at the condominiums. Mine was huge. When you walked in, there was a small but full-size kitchen to the immediate left and a dining room table directly in front. Beyond the dining table was a giant living room with sliding glass doors that opened to the ocean. To the left of the living room was a large separate bedroom and extra large bathroom.

I was standing in the entry and the pilots had gone to check the place out. Directly in front of me was that dining room table. Atop it was a glass with fresh flowers. I looked at that glass, pulled out the flowers and ran to my most beloved pilot and dumped the water over his head. He stood there dumbfounded. Unbeknownst to me, the other pilot had gone into the kitchen, grabbed a pitcher, filled it up with water and threw it all over me. Let the fighting begin, a war was-a-brewing!

My little glass incident escalated into a full blown water fight—a water fight of mammoth proportions. Nothing that held water was unused. Trashcans became coveted artillery.

We ran from condo to condo, hid in closets, propped plastic glasses over doors, it was war—and it was hilarious! We got so carried away I couldn't even sleep in my bed because it was too wet. I had to sleep on the couch. The next day, feeling surprisingly wonderful, we went to sit on the beach. It was such a beautiful beach with some of the whitest sand I had yet to see and warm, bathtub-like water. We laughed and laughed, reminiscing about the night before. I went in the water and somehow got a crab inside my bikini bottom and it bit me about twenty times. Flying home, it was all I could do not to scratch my butt.

Mykonos, Greece

One of my all time favorite days happened in Greece. Paradise Beach is a fabulous beach on the island of Mykonos. This beach has everything: sand that doesn't stick to you—it's more like microscopic pebbles, crystal clear warm water and mouth-watering fresh vine-ripened produce to go with the most delicious gyros I've ever enjoyed. There was ambience all around with people playing board games in the shade and upbeat yet relaxing music in the background. There were exceptionally friendly and good-looking people that seemed genuinely content without a care in the world, except for maybe which delightful entrée to have for lunch that day - and of course, women with no tops on and a large gay population.

After striking up a conversation with a local who lay next

to me on the beach, I was invited on a boat for a day trip to an uninhabited island and volcano caves. I had a feeling that another escapade was about to unfold. There were fourteen people from eight different countries speaking six different languages. Italian/Spanish became the conduit language, it wasn't perfect but it sort of worked through the chain of communication. Although, we really didn't communicate well, it wasn't hugely necessary because what we saw that day left everyone speechless.

The caves, accessible only by boat, were spectacular. The water inside the caves was almost transparent. Abundant sea life was everywhere you looked in every hue. The natural beauty in those caves was indescribable. All six languages were indeed amazed. It was like diving into an animated movie, only this was real. We ate sea urchin, which I don't recommend, salty-yuck, that was pulled right out of the water. We swam and climbed on the rocks while our guide shared his passion of the sea with us, in English!

The only thing to drink on the boat was warm screwdrivers or warm Coors. After the caves, almost everyone decided that a screwdriver was just what we needed to toast our newfound paradise. Then we sped off to another beautiful beach on an island, again - only accessible by boat. We explored the island while our guide prepared our barbecued lunch. That was the best barbecue because everything is so fresh in Mykonos. By this time, no one was feeling any pain from the drinks, and we somehow ended up in a colossal sand fight. I mean colossal! That was another adventure that just sort of happened —must have been the booze! Then we ate and passed out on the beach until our guide awakened us for the trip back. That day will always remain one of the top five days in my life—you know what I mean, days when you are so appreciative you're alive.

Cabo San Lucas, Mexico

It seemed that when I was busy, I was extremely busy and when I was slow, I was dead. I guess that's kind of the way of the world. I was asked to do a five-day charter to Cabo San

Lucas, Mexico. No matter how beat up and tired you are, turning down a Cabo San Lucas trip is just nuts. It's a short flight and a great destination. My passengers turned out to be a group of eight guys going deep-sea fishing..

The chief passenger was a friend of one my owners and I had flown him before. He had just received some sort of windfall and had not only chartered the jet, but a sixty-four foot sport fishing boat, as well. These were great guys, and so much fun it resembled nothing like work. By the time we arrived in Cabo they'd invited me to go out fishing with them. Having enjoyed deep-sea fishing in the past, I didn't hesitate to say yes.

My hotel was in the same vicinity as the marina, so I trekked on down to the boat at 6:45 a.m. ready for a seven o'clock launch. The yacht was very much a fishing boat but with all the amenities of a luxury liner. We set off right on time in search of big fish. After we had been out for a while, all of the sudden all the rods started to scream at the same time. It seems we had trolled right into a school of tuna and they were everywhere, the guys couldn't catch them fast enough. They were almost jumping in the boat, no reel required. Someone stuck a rod in my hand and I tried to remember when to reel in and all that. After a very quick refresher lesson, I caught a tuna as well. The deck hands began to fillet the tuna, they put some on a plate and we ate it right there—now that's fresh fish! We ended up catching over ten tuna, two Dorado (mahi-mahi) and a roosterfish. No marlin, but still some serious bragging rights!

After awhile I headed up to the front of the boat and sat on the gang plank to watch in amazement the flying fish that were leaping out of the water all over the place. Then a couple of stingrays showed up. Then dolphins made an appearance. They swam and jumped all around me; they like to ride the wake at the bow of the boat. I swear they were smiling at me while they were jumping and twirling.

On the way back into the marina, the captain asked me if I wanted to pilot the boat. Are you kidding? I want to drive everything. He gave me a short lesson on what to do which wasn't much other than "head for the arch." I sat on the bridge feeling all sure of myself because I was indeed heading straight for the arch, turning that wheel like a seasoned captain. I did notice it took the boat awhile to "come about" when I turned the gigantic wheel. When I mentioned this to the guys, a few of them began to snicker explaining that the boat was so big that it was normal for it to turn slowly. "Okay." I bought that and continued on my merry way as chief commanding officer.

When we were closing in on the arch, the skipper said he would have to take over as we were coming in close proximity to the beach and other yachts. So I gave up the wheel and all the guys told me what a great job I did. Then they broke out into chuckles that escalated into hearty laughter, hysterical laughter, thigh-slapping laughter. I was puzzled. "What the hell is so dang funny?" And then they confessed the boat was on autopilot the whole way—the morons.

Caracas, Venezuela to Imperial Palace, Japan

One day after flying my passengers to Caracas,

Venezuela and having a lovely layover there, we headed to

Narita, Japan, with a stop in Washington, DC, for a meeting.

Four hours later my passengers re-boarded for the flight back to

Japan. We stopped in Anchorage where we got fuel and changed

pilots. As usual, I stayed with the passengers. When we finally

arrived at the Imperial Palace in Japan, I was dead tired and

cranky. I had been up for almost two days and on my feet for

much of the time.

When I opened my hotel room door to discover a

Japanese room instead of a "Western" room it sent me over the

edge. I stood in my room freaking out! I had a futon instead of a

mattress and after the day I'd just conquered, I damn well

deserved at least a stupid bed! One of my pilots, hearing my

hysteria, came to my room. He calmed me down, pulled a beer

out of the little refrigerator and made me guzzle it. Then he

ordered me into the bathroom to change into my pajamas. That's

when I noticed I didn't have a shower but a strange looking can

of a bathtub-like thing. I guess you sit in it like a toilet only with water and you don't pee. When I emerged, he instructed me to lie down on the futon, and I passed out—for an entire day.

On that same trip, someone had decided we needed to see a Geisha house. I knew what a Geisha was, sort of, but I had no idea what to expect. We all sat down cross-legged on pillows behind this long counter-like table with a small stage in front of us. The Geisha girls came out one at a time and began an elaborate tea ceremony of sorts and when they finally finished, they sat there looking at us.

It was odd because I stared at them more than they stared at me. I thought to myself, *All that white makeup, isn't that bad for your skin? Does that costume Velcro on or do you have to go through all the crap night after night to get it on? Is that a wig or your real hair? And how can you possibly walk in those shoes? Don't your feet hurt? I mean, mine do and I don't have to wear those kind of weird shoes!*

After the tea ceremony, they got up and did this graceful, probably traditional dance. It seemed like they were telling a story although I have no idea what any of it meant, or if it was supposed to mean anything! I don't think that women were normally permitted inside, as guests anyway, because there was not a ladies' restroom. I was relieved to leave. I later learned much more about geishas and how their dance can mean many different things depending on who is performing; there are many misconceptions that date back centuries.

Like this trip hadn't enough drama in it, I decided to go rollerblading. I used to bring my rollerblades everywhere I went. I loved to rollerblade and still do. When I was truly bored, I could always put on my rollerblades and take off, get a little exercise and enjoy the scenery. I had convinced one of my favorite pilots to go rollerblading with me whenever we flew together. Since we were staying at the Imperial Palace Hotel, we decided to head across the street to the Imperial Palace and go rollerblading there. It had lavish spacious gardens and beautiful long concrete paths, the perfect place.

Uh-oh—not so perfect. The Imperial Palace gardens are

sacred and apparently we were destroying that sanction. They were extremely displeased by our choice in desecrating their holy area. I'm certain we would have been arrested or whatever they do to you for a discretion of this nature, but we started fast-talking about who our employer was. I certainly learned a lesson here. Like I said earlier in this chapter, cultural differences can be challenging.

Juneau, Alaska

Another time when I was very happy at home, absorbing the beach and everything it had to offer, I was called for a ten-day flight to Juneau, Alaska. Since it was mid-summer I figured the passengers were going on an Alaskan cruise. I never really knew what the passengers were doing unless they offered up an explanation during the flight. If they were on a cruise that meant the flight crew had the other eight days off—a fantastic layover.

It was an uneventful flight to Juneau, and I learned that the passengers were indeed going on a cruise. We checked into the only decent hotel in Juneau (at least at that time) and began exploring. What were we to do with ourselves for eight days? We decided that we really should see a glacier and some bears or eagles or something, since we were in such close proximity. We learned that to enjoy the best experience we needed to get closer to the actual glaciers. What we would have liked to do was fly our jet to another airport. Although we entertained this idea for a minute, maybe two, for obvious reasons we ditched it. That's when we decided to charter our own little plane!

Ha! What a brainstorm! After we made all the necessary arrangements, we headed back to the airport and climbed inside this cozy little six-seat Cessna 206. It was a turbulent but thoroughly enjoyable flight to a small town named Gustavus, closer to the glaciers. The view from that little airplane was incredible and the natural beauty of the terrain mesmerized me. We took a taxi from the airport to the wharf where we boarded a day boat to take us and maybe fifty or so other people to get up close and personal with a glacier.

If you've never seen a glacier "calve," put it on your

bucket list, because it is spectacular. The ice is shimmering blue, which I think has to do with the absorption of light in thick dense ice, but I'm clearly not a scientist so don't quote me. When it "calves" or a piece breaks off, the sound is undeniable. It's like thunder, like thunder all around you. Depending on how large the chunk that falls in the water, the resulting spray can shoot upwards twice as high as the glacier. It's Mother Nature roaring with power and supremacy. It is a sight that will definitely hold you in reverence of natural beauty, even if you're freezing your arse off. All around us was something to see; little baby sea lions floating around on bits and pieces of glacier ice, momma bears with cubs playing by the edge of the sea, and bald eagles in giant trees (hard to see, but with binoculars definitely a sight to behold).

After a truly invigorating day, we turned and began our journey back to the wharf. Then the weather changed. The sky became dark and the wind began howling and it was cold, really cold, bone-chilling cold. By the time we made our way to the wharf, it was apparent we were not getting back to Juneau that afternoon. We weren't alone, when the weather comes in, in Alaska, you hold tight. So without options that's what we did. The only hotel was completely full and we ended up hanging out in the lobby with many other people. I spent the entire time panicked that the passengers were going to call and want to leave early which would have been impossible because we were stuck in a teeny little town without our jet. As soon as we had a small window of good weather, we left in a hurry.

Cairo, Egypt

I flew the better part of four years for my favorite owner, Jim Williams, chairman and CEO of Golden State Foods, now retired. Based in Southern California, GSF is the second largest food supplier for McDonald's and was integral to the growth of McDonald's. GSF has twelve distribution and production plants in the United States, Australia, and Egypt. I really felt like I hit the jackpot with this flight department; I loved working for Jim Williams, his colleagues, his wife, and their friends, and the pilots and engineer. Incidentally, he is one of Roger Penske's good friends and was a sponsor for one of his racecar teams.

While I was in his employ we began traveling to Egypt for the new bakery and distribution center. The Egyptian military would stand guard at our aircraft every waking minute we were not with it. We had three militia at three different points on the aircraft at all times, one on the nose and one on each wing and engine; an obvious indication that we were in a precarious place.

We stayed at an old-castle-turned-hotel that was really quite fabulous, with many amenities. We were not allowed to drink the water or even brush our teeth with it, nor was it recommended to shave in case of a cut. I brought a case of Evian water with us and passed them out upon landing. The pool was huge, surrounded by a giant patio area and a gym, which was always a favorite pastime of mine. Behind the pool was a little spa where I could get a thirty-minute massage for fifteen US dollars—I frequently took advantage of this.

I would sit by the pool and try using the Spanish/Italian

translation tool to communicate, although in Egypt it wasn't as effective as in Greece. Just for kicks, I decided to call my father while he was at work; he was a Superior court judge at that time. His bailiff interrupted the case he was trying and told him I was on the phone, calling from Egypt. That phone call cost me $125, dumb girl, should have brought him back a $125 present instead! But, he still tells this story, so I guess it was worth it.

When we first began to travel to Egypt, Mr. Williams hired a driver/bodyguard to watch over the crew, as he knew that the flight engineer and I would not stay in our rooms and he was concerned for our welfare—probably his as well. Regardless, we had a car and driver at our disposal. We rode camels to the pyramids, which are truly exquisite and mind-boggling to think that they were created so long ago with what must have been agonizing labor.

From my hotel room window, I could see families living on tiny boats on the Nile. I wondered why they lived on boats when the Nile was so brown and smelly. The families who live on the Nile are fisherman; they live on fish, bread, and tea. The river was brown because of sediment, and the smell was from raw sewage and pollution. It really did stink.

For a shopping experience, we went into the depths of the bazaar; it was a giant maze of shops filled with glass perfume bottles, hookah pipes, authentic Egyptian cotton, and handmade wares of all sorts. The poverty was sickening. If you were caught stealing, they would chop off a hand, caught a second time and the other hand goes. I saw people moving about on skateboards with no hands or feet, it was horrifying.

One thing I used to do with my time on layovers was play roulette. I've played roulette all over the world. I adore it because I don't have to pay close attention, and I like to people watch, especially in a foreign country. My mother taught me a system to play roulette when I was a teenager, and I have been using it ever since. I must confess it works seven times out of ten.

I didn't even realize you could gamble in Egypt, but when I found out there was a casino in the basement of our hotel,

I decided to try my luck. I wasn't just the only American there; I was also the only woman. I thought briefly about leaving because I had this slightly eerie feeling, but I very much was in the mood to play roulette so I stuffed the feeling on a backburner and began to play and then to win.

I won a lot of money and a lot of attention. A gentlemen next to me happened to be a sultan of some sort and was obviously well-respected not only in the casino, but from what I learned later, most of Egypt. He was intrigued by me, my roulette system, and what I was doing in Egypt, in the basement of a very old castle, gambling. He would not stop asking me questions. Eventually he stopped playing and just watched me, perhaps playing the part of my bodyguard.

He asked me if I wanted to go to some exclusive, hotspot bar. A valet delivered a sparkling brand-new Rolls Royce. We drove to the club, a place you can't go unless you're well-connected and not at all if you're an American. The club itself was exquisite, although kind of weird too. There were lots of couches with draperies hanging very low from the ceiling, all decorated in reds and browns. My escort told me all about the great city of Cairo - he was a walking, talking history lesson. The reason all of the above is here is because I learned it from the Sultan. In the middle of my Egyptian culture class, I looked up and there was—you guessed it—my boss, Mr. Williams! I had beaten him to the hotspot. Yikes, time to go…

Sydney, Australia

On another trip with Jim Williams, this one around the Pacific Rim, I was wandering around Sydney, Australia and was drawn to a unique store. I found a five foot giraffe which was hand-carved from African balsawood and is exquisite. After I purchased it, they wrapped it and wrapped it so it looked like a giant cigar and I carried it back to my hotel - which was no easy task – trying to balance the awkward giant cigar on my shoulder.

The next morning when I met the pilots for the taxi ride back to the airport, they weren't too pleased that *that thing* was coming with us. It had to sit across our laps in the back. And then when Mr. Williams, arrived at the airplane ready for the lengthy flight back to the States. He said: "I don't know what the hell that thing is, but if we get stopped at customs in Honolulu, I am going to be pissed." We got stopped, he was pissed. But, not that pissed, I still had a job. (It did take them almost thirty minutes to unwrap it!) I love that giraffe; it has a red bow tie, a broken but glued neck and a permanent home. To be fair, I did purchase a lot of stuff while flying with Jim and GSF. Sometimes the baggage area was packed with my crap. I usually prayed he wouldn't look back there – but he always did!

Singapore, Singapore

On one of my Pacific Rim trips we were getting ready to leave Singapore. Well, we were, the plane was not. The flight engineer could not fix our broken plane without a new part. Well, you know how that goes. We were stuck there waiting for a part to arrive. The passengers took a commercial flight to the next country and we stayed until the part was delivered. I wasn't ready to leave Singapore anyway. It's one of my favorite places.

So, I began to explore every nook and cranny of that island.

When I was growing up, we always went to our favorite lake where everybody waterskied. I still very much enjoy the sport, so I was thoroughly delighted to discover I could go water skiing in Singapore. I jumped into a taxi and was whisked away to the outskirts of the island in the straights between Singapore and Malaysia.

It wasn't much of a beach, more like where the edge of the jungle meets the water. The water was brownish and murky, but scrumptiously warm and flat—razor blade flat, not a ripple of activity. I climbed aboard a dilapidated boat with two locals, donned my life vest, was given an old rope and an even older ski and set off on another adventure. I skied for a long, long while, until I thought my hands were going to be permanently damaged as the handle slid a centimeter at a time down my fingers and eventually, I just could not hold on anymore. It was a perfect and glorious outing, what a fantastic way to spend my time! As I climbed back into the boat, the locals told me it was a good thing

I didn't fall because of all the crocodiles in the water! Uh, excuse me? To this day I do not know if they were joking or not.

By the way, Singapore is also a uniquely situated and a humungous port. The shopping is incredible and Lucky Plaza is a must stop and shop destination when in that country. The same holds true of Panama with all the barges traveling through. If the containers are seized because of incorrect or questionable labels, the items are sold in the local malls at a considerable discount. While in Singapore, I had to buy a new suitcase for all the new clothes, shoes and purses I found at very inexpensive prices. In Panama, I purchased board shorts for my young son for $1.00 per piece and jeans for me for $6.00. Seriously -the shopping is unbelievable!

Side note on Panama: there are many Americans in Panama that are hiding there evading U.S. Income tax. It is an unincorporated US territory and is known as a "flag of convenience", making it an ideal tax haven. 2008 Presidential Candidate John McCain was born here in 1936 - his eligibility to run for US President was questioned and obviously answered in his favor.

One time when we arrived at the Marriott, there was a gentleman in the lobby; I would almost bet he was waiting for other Americans to show up. He was the one who took us all over that fine city. So, if you're in Panama – look around the lobby, make friends. You might get a suitcase full of cheap clothes out of it!

One other thing about Singapore: it is home to a statue of a lion head and a mermaid tail at the entrance to the magnificent harbor. This "merlion" is the symbol of the country and quite prevalent within it. It shoots a fountain of water out of its mouth and is very cool to see on arrival, especially at night.

Toluca, Mexico

An unusual place I frequented in the early 1990s was Toluca, Mexico. I found the most amazing shoe place in Toluca. It was maybe a half square mile of shoe stands. This was during the era of cowboy boots, and they had some outrageously unique ones. All kinds of weird skins I'd never seen before. The prices were so cheap. I couldn't believe my luck. GSF had business in Toluca, and we went there often. I decided to bring back cowboy boots for everyone, but the sizes were wacky. When I was home,

I would trace the person's foot I was buying for and take the

traced footprint and measure it to the boot. It worked most of the time but not always. I also bought loads of leather coats and belts and purses, what a coup!

Of course, you have to watch your exchange rate. One needs a pocket calculator unless you're with one of those pilots who can tell you the cost in dollars lickety- split, and is willing to trail behind you, a walking, talking calculator—gotta love these guys!

Chapter 6: Welcome to Life on the Road

The Perks of Being a Private Flight Attendant

I have flown with all kinds of people. Most of them were courteous and kind. Most of them were fabulous passengers but didn't do much beyond that. But some of them did. If I was flying full time for a corporation then I was part of the family, so to speak, and was treated as such. If I was an independent contractor but still worked every trip, then I was usually part of the family as well. If I was the regular flight attendant on a jet with infrequent passengers, then the passengers knew they were going to see me and were typically pleased. And if it was a charter, no one knew anyone, but no one could have been someone!

Sometimes, I received some amazing benefits. For instance, one of our flights had a name like Joe Smith or something and he turned out to be a famous producer. The rampers accidently took my luggage off the airplane with the producers and loaded it into the limousine. Once I figured out my bag was missing, we had to drive to his house in New Jersey to retrieve it. Feeling terrible about the inconvenience, he gave us three front row seats to a Broadway show.

I was given tickets to all kinds of events: grand openings, famous comedy shows, concerts, as well as legendary sports and golf tournaments. I was also given reservations at famous supper houses when the owners' plans would change and they couldn't go. They would even pick up the tab, albeit, by expense report.

I had an owner who would obtain tickets for us to Broadway shows in New York when no one could get tickets to "the" play of the time. He also acquired tickets to the hottest shows in Las Vegas. The seats were always great, and it always made us feel special.

One time we stayed at the Waldorf Astoria in New York to babysit the luggage. The passengers were going directly from the airplane to some event and couldn't check in right away. I made sure their baggage was in their room and clothing hung in the closet. The perks of that—a weekend at the Waldorf!

Jim Williams, at Golden State Foods, would put us up at his hotel when we were out of the country, he didn't want us to get sick. On the way to Egypt, we would have to overnight somewhere for crew rest. We stayed in some amazing airport hotels in countries like Sweden and Switzerland. Incidentally, he also gave me a lapel pin that allowed me to go anywhere inside any Indy Car circuit race, even to the pits.

I was headed to Las Vegas for a long weekend—a trip I had flown dozens of times—and was given tickets to an Eagles concert. I wasn't familiar with the venue and had no idea where it was located in relation to my hotel. It turned out to be a well-worn outdoor arena reminiscent of a fairground with bench-like seating. It was sizzling hot, so hot you began to sweat as soon as you entered the stadium even though it was at night. I checked my ticket and made my way towards the stage to a seat smack dab in the middle of the twelfth row. Everyone was dancing on their seats and hooting and hollering. I had never seen the Eagles perform live, and this will remain the best concert I have ever seen, heat and all. The only bummer was they ran out of beer, but the beer was warm anyway.

On another long weekend in Vegas, Jim Williams' wife, Toni, found out it was my birthday. She instructed me to go to the spa in our hotel because she had arranged a birthday present. I went to the spa as soon as we arrived and, to my sincere delight and amazement, I learned she had purchased a massage and facial for me! When she boarded the airplane for our return to Southern California she had presents for me too, elaborately wrapped, the whole nine yards. How many times can you say thank you without becoming annoying?

And yet again, I received a call for a charter flight leaving out of Las Vegas. We were to deadhead to Las Vegas, pick up a passenger and drop him in San Francisco—an easy money flight. We repositioned in Vegas and waited for our passenger at the FBO. When our passenger boarded the plane, he exclaimed his delight with the plane and us. Apparently he was under the impression we were taking him all the way to his home country of Malaysia. He was one of the world's leading Baccarat players and had lost a few million at Caesars Palace. He had assumed Caesars would foot the bill for his ride home, not just to San Francisco, but all the way to Malaysia.

I was not planning on having dinner in Malaysia that night. I was planning on having dinner in Newport Beach. The pilots assumed they'd be home for dinner too. We went through some intense chaos, massive panicky phone calls and confusion for the next hour or so while we tried to explain to him that we didn't have passports, another pilot, or catering. We finally talked our gambling guru into taking the commercial flight out of San Francisco. While airborne I only served him an orange juice. When we arrived in San Francisco, he gave me a $500 tip. Like I said—easy money.

I also had one gentleman who owned a share in an airplane with two other men. Sometimes, a group of people or corporations will join together and share a jet. This will obviously offset the exorbitant costs and is a great arrangement if you don't travel a huge amount. (There are now mega-companies that do this and they are very popular.) One of the co-owners used to tip the pilots and me one hundred dollars every day we flew. He loved to tease us with his hundred dollar bills, sometimes hiding them in the airplane. After he deplaned he would tell me that he forgot his sunglasses, when I went to find them, I would find three hundred dollar bills instead! Sometimes he would act like he forgot to tip us, deplane, climb into his waiting limo and shut the door to leave. Then he would jump out holding the bills. The feisty old guy was so much fun to fly for, always smiling and cheerful, planning his mischief.

I was friends with a few other flight attendants in the industry who had the same advantages as me. Sometimes we would end up in the same city at the same time. Although rarely, when it did happen, it was fun! It was wonderful to be with my friends for a change. This girlfriend was Arnold Schwarzenegger and Maria Shriver's flight attendant. She was on the island of Maui for the opening of the Planet Hollywood in Lahaina (since closed). I was there with Golden State Foods for a vacation. She asked me if I wanted to tag along to the grand opening. It was truly a red carpet event—a red carpet all the way up Front Street -the main street in Lahaina, Maui-leading into Planet Hollywood. She and I had a marvelous good time with the likes of Demi Moore, Bruce Willis, Sylvester Stallone, and of course Arnold and Maria.

I also heard stories from my pilots. Again, I wasn't the only flight attendant in the corporate aviation industry. I remember one of them telling me about a flight attendant who was asked to pass a mirror (for cocaine) around from passenger to passenger. I also remember them telling me that there were times when the marijuana smoke was so thick in the cabin that they were worried they may actually be getting high. By the way, as a general rule; the pilots do not like flying rock stars but the flight attendants usually can't wait!

One of the pilots told me a story, while we were on the way to Europe and had an ocean of time to kill. They had done a charter for an infrequent customer, without his wife, but with strippers. It was a bachelor party and the owner had taken his soon to be son-in-law on the ride of his life. Apparently, the boys got hammered and the strippers were the entertainment. Nice *welcome to the family* gift? The pilots are on "auto pilot" for most of every flight, so on this flight, they were thoroughly distracted! Then the future son-in-law did something that the father-in-law didn't like and they began to shout at one another. Now, the others got involved and the shouting escalated into screaming cussing matches. Then fists began to fly around the cabin. And then grown men began to fly around the cabin. The pilots had to land to save the airplane. They were considerably worried about their safety, the passengers' safety and the destruction of the interior of the aircraft. Again, the problems of flying the rich and famous!

I never had anything bizarre like that happen, but I did

reciprocate a time or two myself. I knew one CEO who liked to waterski and since my parents had a house on a lake and a boat on the water in front of it, I offered to take him and his son waterskiing. One of our pilots flew this CEO in a Cessna 172 to a small airport by my parents' house. I picked him up and took him to my parents' home where we skied and played in the boat all day. While feeding my guest his favorite lunch, I received a call from the pilot who explained that the little airplane was having a mechanical issue. The CEO told them to send another plane to pick him up because he had a golf tee time to make and he didn't want to be late! Ah—the benefits of having your own flight department...

Allow me to share some of the not-so-good-times. Let's talk about winter. Winter sucks. When you're flying in snow and ice, there are always issues. First and foremost is being cold, or trying to get warm when you're freezing your ass off and maintain a jovial mood. Then there are diversions (diversions create a snowball effect of countless other issues) and de-icing delays and hangar concerns and water problems and so, so many other complications.

I'll start with the all the extra luggage everyone brings. I mean wow! Some passengers may be going skiing for the weekend and bring three steamer trunks of crap with them, because God forbid, they wouldn't have the matching accessories to the fifth-choice outfit. If they are on a ski holiday, chances are the airport is located in a high altitude, meaning we have weight issues. Well, we have weight issues if you plan on returning—the heavier the airplane, the harder it is to take off in high altitude. So pardon me if your third trunk gets left behind. In Aspen, Colorado, we will only fuel the aircraft enough to take off and get to another airport to fuel for the length of the trip – weight is a *huge* issue in high altitude.

I once had a flight to Aspen with nine male passengers and nine snowboards. With all the extra luggage, we ended up having to put three snowboards in the lavatory! That was a hoot, getting into the lavatory by pushing the door open hard enough so the snowboards would swing to the other side by the baggage door. Not FAA approved I'm sure.

We had to live with the snowboard situation because we had no alternative. But people still don't get the fact that you can't put stuff anywhere or everywhere. Even if you are paying the tab and even if it is a private jet, it is still an airplane, and, frankly, I don't want your twenty-five pound briefcase flying through the cabin and hitting the pilot in the head because he's my ride home, thank you very much.

If we overnight in a city where the temperature drops below freezing, and there's not a *heated* hangar that someone paid big bucks for—then you're screwed. The jet has to sit outside overnight - so the flight attendant must remove every item from that airplane that might freeze. This can be an amazing amount of stock depending on who, what, or where you're flying. If you leave one soda can onboard and it freezes, it will explode and make a huge and costly mess. It's extremely difficult to get frozen soda out of a suede side runner. Ever diligent, you must purge all the water in the aircraft on descent. One time I opened the toilet to discover a giant chunk of blue ice, we were lucky to melt it but it could have been disastrous.

Removing freezable items is in addition to the normal trash removal, perishable removal, dirty dish removal, cleaning, and vacuuming. The icing on the cake here is the ice on the tarmac. Now I'm walking in the freezing rain/snow/sleet in high heels mind you, to the FBO, which may be a football field away from the airplane.

Now let's talk reverse. The airplane is always severely colder or warmer than the outside temperature. I have to put all that stock back on the aircraft along with the catering, perishables, and dishes. It was so cold in Detroit once, I slipped on the ice walking out to the airplane and fell on my butt. I thought my fingers were frozen because I couldn't open the drawers in the galley. I cried. I mean it was so cold that my fingers wouldn't work.

There are also hazards of being in unfamiliar spaces.

Awakening or leaving your hotel room and not remembering where you are, what are you supposed to be doing today, what day is it anyway? Where are the elevators? Or not knowing where your room is located—no idea. Putting your key in the lock only to discover it's the key from two hotels ago. I've also randomly put my key in any door hoping one will open—after all I was in the general vicinity. I've called down to the front desk plenty of times to ask what room I was in – I've also called my pilots to ask them. I've unlocked my room only to disturb the sleeping occupant - this just sucks. Or not being able to find your hotel at all! I was so lost in Mykonos and in Barcelona I had to hire a taxi to find the hotel. Or trying to find the rental car after getting to the hotel late and exhausted the night before. What kind of car did we get? No idea. Hit the unlock button on the key fob until you hear or see a car bleeping...

We also have random problems. Aircraft computer malfunction: control, alt, delete airplane (turn airplane off completely and restart) when you're sitting at the runway ready to takeoff—with fourteen planes behind you - that's always fun...

If one takes the time to stop and smell the jet fuel, it's amazing what you'll notice. I will never forget landing in Hong Kong and having every sense lit up all at once, or studying the horizon while the sun is setting waiting for the green flash. Or admiring the view of Panama as we climb after takeoff, wondering what it must have been like to dredge the canal and how the completion of it changed the world. Or landing at dusk in a sea of lightening bugs in Wisconsin. Or taking off from Sydney, Australia, at sunset, one of the most picturesque cities in the world, while recalling it started out as a derelict dump. Or watching a volcano—in all its fierceness—erupt at night. Or looking out the window in the middle of the Atlantic in the dead of night and appreciating the dark. Or waiting for the airplane to break out of the clouds, which are like giant cotton balls, and then being mesmerized by them. Or watching a thunder and lightning storm from the airplane and being so captivated, truly lost in thoughts. When you take yourself out of yourself you can see the splendor of where you are.

Ciao, au revoir, sayonara, adios, auf wiedersehen, ta-ta, arrivederci, ma'a salama, zai-jian, antio, totsiens, aloha, and mahola!

Made in the USA
Lexington, KY
13 October 2015